CW01572890

EVERTON

– THE 25 YEAR RECORD

1974-75 to 1998-99

SEASON BY SEASON WRITE-UPS
David Powter

EDITOR
Michael Robinson

British Library Cataloguing in Publication Data

A catalogue record for this book is available from the British Library

ISBN 1-86223-042-0

Printed by The Cromwell Press

CONTENTS

The F.A. Cup bedecked in Everton's colours
after the 1994/95 triumph.

EVERTON F.C.
– Seasons 1974-75 to 1998-99

Everton finished in the bottom half of the table for the seventh time in eight campaigns in 1998-99. Walter Smith's side showed just enough improvement late in the campaign to edge clear of relegation in 14th place. Twenty five seasons earlier, though, Everton were one of the most consistent and well respected sides in the country.

The man at the helm in 1974-75 was Billy Bingham, who saw his side start the campaign in commanding form. They lost just once during the first half of the season and, although criticised for their negative and over aggressive attitude, they appeared to be good bets for the title with only ten games remaining. However, a 3-0 defeat at struggling Carlisle climaxed a jittery spell, during which they took only two points from four games. Consequently, the fast finishing Derby County, Liverpool and Ipswich Town all went past the Toffeemen, whose only consolation was fourth place and qualification for the UEFA Cup.

Their European adventure in 1975-76 was a brief one as they were bundled out by a solitary penalty in Milan, after Internazionale had held them to a goalless draw at Goodison Park. In the League, Bingham's men never recovered from an opening day 4-1 home defeat by Coventry City and it took a closing run of three successive victories to lift them to a flattering 11th place.

In January 1977, only 20 months after nearly steering Everton to the title, Billy Bingham lost his job. Relegation was a distinct possibility when new manager Gordon Lee arrived in February; however, his side lost only two of their last 18 fixtures to finish comfortably in ninth spot. Everton showed fine cup form in 1976-77 but ultimately met double despair in the city of Manchester.

They conceded just one goal en route to a League Cup final meeting with Aston Villa. The Wembley game finished goalless and the two sides could still not be separated after sharing two goals at Hillsborough. Another 120 minutes of tight football followed, before Villa finally ran out 3-2 winners at Old Trafford.

Exactly two weeks later, Evertonians' hearts were broken on the other side of the city as their team lost 3-0 to Liverpool in an F.A. Cup semi-final replay. The initial tie, also held at Maine Road, ended 2-2.

Despite losing the opening two games of 1977-78, Lee's side picked up momentum with an unbeaten run of 18 games. However, any realistic hopes of making a serious tilt at the title were crushed when Manchester United romped to a 6-2 victory at Goodison Park on Boxing Day, followed by another reverse at Leeds a day later. The Toffeemen never got back on terms with Nottingham Forest (who finished as comprehensive Champions) and another sticky patch in April – when they slid to three more defeats – cost them the runners-up spot (to Liverpool) and they finished third. Bob Latchford netted 30 times to be the First Division's leading scorer in 1977-78. It was the fourth successive campaign that the big striker had headed the club's list of scorers.

The two Merseyside giants dominated the early stages of 1978-79. Liverpool led the way with ten wins out of eleven; but Everton kept pace with an unbeaten record until losing narrowly at Coventry just before Christmas. Lee's side faded out of contention afterwards though and eventually had to be content with fourth place.

Earlier in 1978-79 Everton enjoyed themselves by twice hammering Finn Harps 5-0 in the UEFA Cup first round. However, they perished in the next round on away goals to Dukla Prague. Lee's side also had one glorious evening in the League Cup, with an 8-0 annihilation of Wimbledon. Latchford netted five against the Dons, who were then a Fourth Division side.

Everton's fortunes took a further dip in 1979-80. They exited the UEFA Cup to Feyenoord in the first round, but performed even worse in the League, winning only five times in the first half of the season and just four more times in the second half. Two of those victories were crucial ones in April, though, ensuring relegation was avoided by four points. Even so, a final finish of 19th was Everton's worst since they regained their top-flight status in 1955. Gordon Lee would probably have paid the price with his job but for his side's fine F.A. Cup run. It was Second Division West Ham United, the eventual winners, who denied them a Wembley place with an extra-time winner in a semi-final replay at Elland Road.

Another good F.A. Cup run followed in 1980-81, before Lee's men ran out of steam in another replay, this time at the quarter-final stage against Manchester City. Everton's League form was very uneven in 1980-81: they won six games on the trot in the autumn; but then won only six of their last 32 games to finish 15th.

Lee was dismissed in May 1981, after just over four years in charge, and replaced by player-manager Howard Kendall. Lee had brought some improvements to Goodison, especially in the defensive department; but not for the first time in his career it was felt he was unable to get the best out of the star performers.

Kendall (who quickly hung up his boots) laid the groundwork for future successes in his first season at the helm when Gary Stevens, Neville Southall (signed from Bury), Kevin Richardson, Graeme Sharp (signed from Dumbarton) and Adrian Heath (signed from Stoke City) all made their Everton debuts. Five victories and a draw in the last six games underlined their improvement and they finished 1981-82 in eighth place.

Another late flourish, when they won six of their last eight games, lifted the Toffeemen one place to seventh in 1982-83. Any chance of F.A. Cup glory evaporated with a narrow defeat at Old Trafford in the quarter-final.

Kendall's job appeared to be very much on the line during the course of 1983-84. By mid-January his side had sunk to 18th place and looked destined to exit the Milk Cup at Oxford. Yet Everton rallied, won a replay and completely turned around their season. They gradually climbed the table and finished seventh. Their run in the Milk Cup eventually turned sour when Liverpool beat them 1-0 in a final replay at Maine Road; however, glory and their first trophy in 14 years, was just around the corner. The Toffeemen stuck to their task in the F.A. Cup, and Sharp and Andy Gray netted the goals which punctured Watford's dreams in the final.

Without a shadow of doubt, 1984-85 was the finest season in the history of Everton FC. The Toffeemen romped to the League Championship, 13 points ahead of runners-up Liverpool. Their record haul of 90 points would have been even higher but for three defeats in their final four fixtures, when the title was already secured. Everton also enjoyed a marvellous European campaign, culminating in a memorable May evening in Rotterdam when Gray, Trevor Steven and Kevin Sheedy scored in a 3-1 victory over Rapid Vienna in the Cup Winners' Cup final. Only a magnificent curling strike by Manchester United's Norman Whiteside crushed their hopes of a unique treble in extra-time of the F.A. Cup final.

Awards and plaudits flowed in to Goodison from all directions. Kendall was Manager of the Year, goalkeeper Neville Southall was the Football Writers' Footballer of the Year and midfielder Peter Reid took the Players' Player of the Season award. Southall, Reid, Stevens, Steven, Sharp, Gray, Sheedy, Pat Van Den Hauwe, Paul Bracewell and Kevin Ratcliffe all received international recognition from their respective countries; while consistent centre-half Derek Mountfield (who contributed 10 League goals) was very unlucky to miss out on full international honours.

Events involving the other Liverpool club at the Heysel Stadium prevented Everton returning to Europe for a crack at the senior competition in 1985-86. Gray was replaced up front by a youthful Gary Lineker from Leicester. Lineker's only season at Goodison proved fruitful enough as he netted 38 times, including 30 in the League to top the First Division's list. However, those goals were not quite enough to retain the Championship as Liverpool won a tight three cornered fight that also featured West Ham. Everton defeated the Hammers in the final game to collect second place, two points behind Kenny Dalglish's team.

Liverpool also pipped their neighbours in the F.A. Cup final, netting three times in the second half after Lineker had given Everton the lead.

It was the blue half of Merseyside which enjoyed another Championship success in 1986-87, in spite of Lineker's departure for Barcelona. Due to a series of injuries, Kendall was forced to call upon 23 different players (with only Ratcliffe being ever-present); but in a fine all-round performance Everton finished nine points clear of second placed Liverpool. The goals were spread around with 16 different scorers: Steven top scored with 14 – all but four of which were from the spot.

After bringing four major trophies to Goodison Park, Howard Kendall surprised everybody by leaving for Athletic Bilbao during the summer of 1987. His assistant Colin Harvey stepped up to become manager.

Everton made a stuttering start in defence of their title; but five straight wins early in the new year improved their position. Nevertheless they still finished 20 points behind Liverpool in fourth place. It was the Anfield men who also ended their 1987-88 F.A. Cup hopes in the fourth round, while they exited to Arsenal at the semi-final stage of the Littlewoods Cup.

In a bid to improve his side's scoring rate, Harvey paid West Ham £2 million for Tony Cottee in the summer of 1988. Cottee immediately obliged with 13 goals to be the club's top scorer in 1988-89. However, mediocre League form meant that Everton slipped down the table to finish eighth; although, there was the consolation of two Wembley Cup finals. Both were thrilling affairs but both ended in Everton defeats. Nottingham Forest were victors in the Simod Cup final 4-3, while – much more heartbreakingly – it was Liverpool who yet again got the better of them in the F.A. Cup final by the odd goal in five.

Everton improved two places to finish sixth in 1989-90 and, but for an end of season blip, when they failed to win any of their last three fixtures, they might have finished third.

The Toffeemen made a dismal start to the 1990-91 campaign and were struggling in the lower reaches when Howard Kendall reclaimed his managerial chair in November 1990. Harvey reverted to his old assistant-manager role. League form improved gradually and an unbeaten six game run at the end of the season enabled them to claw their way up to ninth. Everton also enjoyed some cup success but failed to gain a trophy. Crystal Palace beat them in the Zenith Data Systems Cup final at Wembley and West Ham knocked them out of the F.A. Cup at the quarter-final stage.

The arrival of Peter Beardsley raised Goodison Park spirits in 1991-92, but Kendall's side failed to overcome a sluggish start – when they won just once in eight games – and finished 12th.

In terms of their League position, Everton only slipped one place to 13th in 1992-93; however, that is far from the full story. They only finished four points ahead of the third relegated club (Crystal Palace) and would have been even more uncomfortably placed but for a 5-2 victory at Maine Road on the final day of the campaign.

Evertonian pulses were beating even faster twelve months later when they had an even narrower escape from relegation. Kendall (and Harvey) had parted company with the club in January 1994 and Mike Walker was enticed from Norwich to become the new manager. Walker looked likely to be the first manager since Cliff Britton (in 1951) to take Everton down into the second-flight when his side reached the final game of 1993-94 at home to Wimbledon with their fate out of their own hands. A see-saw turn of events elsewhere eventually meant that, by turning around a 2-0 deficit to win 3-2, Everton survived (by two points) in 17th place.

An appalling start to the following season, when they mustered just eight points during the first third of the campaign, cost Walker his job after less than nine months at the helm. Popular former striker Joe Royle moved into the Goodison hot-seat, signalling his intentions by immediately engineering a victory over Liverpool. Royle's side gradually climbed up the table; however, it was not until the penultimate fixture of 1994-95 that Everton sealed their safety.

Meanwhile Everton recorded a string of victories in the F.A. Cup. The club's record £4.3 million signing Duncan Ferguson was a major influence up front, but he was unavailable for the semi-final clash with Tottenham Hotspur at Elland Road. The Londoners were considered favourites, but Royle's men out-played them to win 4-1. Nigerian striker Daniel Amokachi came off the bench to bag a brace.

The Merseysiders again started as under-dogs in the final against Manchester United; but Royle's tactics were spot-on and Paul Rideout's first half header proved enough to give Everton the F.A. Cup for the fifth time in their history. The triumph was also the passport for the club's first European adventure in eleven years.

Sadly, that Cup Winners' Cup run in 1995-96 only embraced four games. After knocking out KR Reykjavik, the Toffeemen slipped out 1-0, on aggregate, to Feyenoord.

After winning only two of their first 11 fixtures, Everton showed greatly improved League form in 1995-96 and finished sixth. Andrei Kanchelskis's arrival from Manchester United proved to be the catalyst and the winger finished top scorer, with 16 goals.

For the second consecutive campaign, lower Division sides (York City and Bradford City) knocked Everton out of both domestic cup competitions in 1996-97. Joe Royle's side spent most of the first part of the season in the top half of the table but six successive defeats around the turn of the year restricted their progress. Royle left the club, by mutual consent, towards the end of March and Watson steered the ship in a caretaker player-manager role. With only one win from their last eight games, Everton slid to 15th place – finishing only two points above relegated Sunderland.

Howard Kendall embarked on his third spell as Everton manager in the summer of 1997. His side made a poor start, winning only three of their first 18 fixtures. Three successive victories around the turn of the year moved them into mid table but another slump took them to the edge of the cliff again. By the final round of games they were precariously placed in the relegation zone, but a home draw against Coventry edged them to safety above Bolton Wanderers (who lost their final fixture) on goal difference. For the second successive campaign, Ferguson was the leading scorer with 11 goals (one more than his tally in 1996-97).

Everton did lift one trophy in 1997-98 when their youngsters defeated Blackburn Rovers in the F.A. Youth Cup final. Among the many jewels in the youth squad was Danny Cadamarteri, who had made a big impact during his run in the first team earlier in the term.

Kendall's third spell at the Goodison helm ended in the summer of 1998 with former Rangers boss Walter Smith taking his place. For much of 1998-99 Smith's side struggled in front of goal. Their first home goal did not come until the end of October and they only found the net three times in their first 12 Goodison fixtures. The mid-February 5-0 home victory over Middlesbrough relieved the drought, but it was the on-loan signing of striker Kevin Campbell which effectively ensured the Toffeemen's safety. Campbell, who ended up top scorer with 8 goals, netted in each of four crucial victories in the spring which enabled Smith's side to finish in 14th place – seven points above the relegation line.

Everton enjoyed some success in the F.A. Cup, defeating Bristol City, Ipswich Town and Coventry City before exiting 4-1 at Newcastle in the quarter-finals. Injuries seriously blighted the club in 1998-99, with new signing John Collins one of several senior players forced to sit out most of the campaign. Many fans were outraged when skipper Ferguson was sold to Newcastle for £8 million, but among the positive pointers for the future was the high level of consistency shown by some of the home-grown crop – most notably Michael Ball and Francis Jeffers. It is the likes of these youngsters that Everton hope will flourish alongside the experienced heads of Collins and Campbell (who signed permanently in the summer of 1999) as Walter Smith reshapes his squad for the future.

1974-75

1	Aug	17	(h)	Derby Co	D	0-0		42,293
2		20	(h)	Stoke C	W	2-1	Royle 2 (1 pen)	35,817
3		24	(a)	West Ham U	W	3-2	Royle (pen), Latchford, Harvey	22,486
4		28	(a)	Stoke C	D	1-1	Latchford	27,954
5		31	(h)	Arsenal	W	2-1	Latchford 2	42,438
6	Sep	7	(a)	Ipswich T	L	0-1		23,393
7		14	(h)	Wolves	D	0-0		36,875
8		21	(a)	Coventry C	D	1-1	Latchford	15,217
9		24	(a)	Q.P.R.	D	2-2	Latchford, Pearson	16,638
10		28	(h)	Leeds U	W	3-2	Seargeant, Lyons, Clements	41,824
11	Oct	5	(h)	Newcastle U	D	1-1	Buckley	40,000
12		12	(a)	Sheffield U	D	2-2	Lyons, Buckley	23,655
13		15	(h)	West Ham U	D	1-1	Lyons	31,882
14		19	(h)	Chelsea	D	1-1	Jones	35,806
15		26	(a)	Burnley	D	1-1	Jones	22,599
16	Nov	2	(h)	Manchester C	W	2-0	Connolly, Jones	43,905
17		9	(a)	Tottenham H	D	1-1	Connolly	29,052
18		16	(h)	Liverpool	D	0-0		57,190
19		30	(h)	Birmingham C	W	4-1	Jones, Dobson, Lyons, Connolly	38,369
20	Dec	7	(a)	Leicester C	W	2-0	Hurst, Telfer	21,451
21		14	(a)	Derby Co	W	1-0	Latchford	24,891
22		21	(h)	Carlisle U	L	2-3	Latchford 2	33,489
23		26	(a)	Wolves	L	0-2		33,120
24		28	(h)	Middlesbrough	D	1-1	Latchford	41,105
25	Jan	11	(h)	Leicester C	W	3-0	Jones, Pearson, Lyons	31,985
26		18	(a)	Birmingham C	W	3-0	Styles (og), Latchford 2	32,284
27		1	(h)	Tottenham H	W	1-0	Pearson	40,912
28		8	(a)	Manchester C	L	1-2	Horswill (og)	44,718
29		22	(a)	Liverpool	D	0-0		55,853
30		25	(h)	Luton T	W	3-1	Telfer, Dobson, Latchford	35,714
31	Mar	1	(a)	Arsenal	W	2-0	Dobson, Lyons	32,216
32		8	(h)	Q.P.R.	W	2-1	Lyons, Latchford	39,567
33		15	(a)	Leeds U	D	0-0		50,084
34		18	(a)	Middlesbrough	L	0-2		32,813
35		22	(h)	Ipswich T	D	1-1	Lyons	46,269
36		29	(a)	Carlisle U	L	0-3		16,049
37		31	(h)	Coventry C	W	1-0	Dobson	39,770
38	Apr	4	(h)	Burnley	D	1-1	Latchford	46,882
39		9	(a)	Luton T	L	1-2	Latchford	13,437
40		12	(a)	Newcastle U	W	1-0	Dobson	29,585
41		19	(h)	Sheffield U	L	2-3	Smallman, Jones (pen)	38,348
42		26	(a)	Chelsea	D	1-1	Latchford	28,432

FINAL LEAGUE POSITION: 4th in Division One

Appearances

Sub. Appearances

Goals

Lawson	Bernard	Seargeant	Clements	Kenyon	Hurst	Buckley	Harvey	Royle	Latchford	Connolly	Darracott	Lyons	Dobson	Davies	Kenny	Pearson	Jones	McLaughin	Telfer	Irving	Scott	McNaught	Marshall	Smallman	
1	2	3	4	5	6	7	8	9	10	11															1
1		3	4	5	6	7	8*	9	10	11	2	12													2
1		3	4		6	7	8	9	10	11	2	5													3
1		3	4		6	7	8	9	10	11	2	5													4
1		3	4	5	6*	7		9	10	11	2	12	8												5
1		3	4	5		7		9	10	11	2	6	8												6
1	2	3	4	5		7		9	10	11		6	8												7
	2	3	11	5		6			10	12		4	8	1	7*	9									8
	2	3	11	5		6			10	12		4	8	1	7*	9									9
	2	3	6	5	12	7			10*	11		4	8	1		9									10
	2	3	6	5		7			10	11		4	8	1		9									11
	2	3	6	5	12	7			10*	11		4	8	1		9									12
	2	3	6	5		7	10			11		4	8	1		9									13
	2	3	6	5	4	7				11		10	8	1		9*	12								14
	2	3		5	6	7*				11		9	8	1		10	4	12							15
	2	3	4	5	6	7				11		9	8	1		10									16
	2	3	4	5	6	7				11		9	8	1		10									17
	2	3	4	5	6	7*				11		9	8	1		12	10								18
	2	3	4	5	6				10	11		9	8	1			7								19
	2	3	4	5	6				10	11		9	8*	1			7		12						20
	2	3	4	5	6				10	11		9		1		12	7		8*						21
	2	3	4	5	6	12			10	11		9		1			7		8*						22
	2	3*	4	5	6	8			10	11		9		1		12	7								23
	2		4	5*		8			10	11		6		1			7	3	12	9					24
			4	5					10			8		1		9	7*	3	11		2	6	12		25
	12		3	5		8*			10			4		1		9			11		2	6	7		26
		3	4	5					10			9	8	1		12			11		2	6	7*		27
	12	3	4	5					10			9	8	1		7			11		2*	6			28
	2	3	4	5	6			9				10	8	1		12	7		11*						29
	2	3	4	5	6	12			10			9	8	1			7		11*						30
	2	3	4	5	6	7			10			9	8	1					11						31
	2	3	4	5	6	7*			10			9	8	1		12			11						32
	2	3	4	5	6				10			9	8	1			7		11						33
	2	3	4*	5	6				10			9	8	1		12	7		11						34
		3	4	5	6	7			10			9		1		8	11				2				35
		3	4*	5	6	7			10			9	8	1		12	11				2				36
	2	3		5	6	4		9				10	8	1		12	7		11*						37
	2	3*	12	5	6	4		9				10	8	1			7		11						38
	2	3		5	6	4		9					8	1		11	7							10	39
	2	3		5	6	4		9					8	1		11	7		12					10*	40
	2	3		5	6	4		9					8	1		11*	7		12					10	41
	2	3		5	6	4		9				8		1		11	7							10	42
7	31	35	39	40	29	31	4	8	36	22	5	36	30	35	2	17	25	2	11	1	6	4	2	4	
	2		1		2	2				2		2				9	1	1	4				1		
		1	1		1	2	1	3	17	3		8	5			3	6		2					1	

1975-76

1	Aug	16	(h)	Coventry C	L	1-4	Kenyon	32,343
2		19	(a)	Burnley	D	1-1	Smallman	20,069
3		23	(a)	Birmingham C	W	1-0	Smallman	26,814
4		26	(h)	Sheffield U	W	3-0	Smallman (pen), Lyons, Latchford	25,846
5		30	(h)	Derby Co	W	2-0	Lyons, Latchford	32,483
6	Sep	6	(a)	Norwich C	L	2-4	Latchford, Pearson	19,672
7		13	(h)	Newcastle U	W	3-0	Latchford, Lyons, Clements	28,938
8		20	(a)	Arsenal	D	2-2	G. Jones, Buckley	24,864
9		27	(h)	Liverpool	D	0-0		55,769
10	Oct	4	(a)	West Ham U	W	1-0	G. Jones	31,985
11		11	(a)	Q.P.R.	L	0-5		23,435
12		18	(h)	Aston Villa	W	2-1	G. Jones 2 (1 pen)	30,376
13		25	(a)	Wolves	W	2-1	Dobson, G. Jones	20,063
14	Nov	1	(h)	Leicester C	D	1-1	Smallman (pen)	24,930
15		8	(a)	Stoke C	L	2-3	Telfer, Pearson	24,677
16		15	(h)	Manchester C	D	1-1	Telfer	32,077
17		22	(a)	Aston Villa	L	1-3	Telfer	33,949
18		29	(a)	Leeds U	L	2-5	Clements (pen), Latchford	30,879
19	Dec	6	(h)	Ipswich T	D	3-3	Dobson 2, Latchford	24,601
20		10	(a)	Tottenham H	D	2-2	Telfer, Latchford	18,638
21		13	(h)	Birmingham C	W	5-2	Latchford, G. Jones, Dobson, Hamilton, Telfer	20,188
22		19	(a)	Coventry C	W	2-1	G. Jones (pen), Latchford	14,419
23		23	(h)	Manchester U	D	1-1	Latchford	41,732
24		27	(a)	Middlesbrough	D	1-1	Latchford	29,275
25	Jan	10	(a)	Newcastle U	L	0-5		31,726
26		17	(h)	Norwich C	D	1-1	Dobson	23,164
27		31	(h)	Burnley	L	2-3	Hamilton 2	21,389
28	Feb	7	(a)	Sheffield U	D	0-0		20,113
29		21	(a)	Manchester C	L	0-3		33,148
30		24	(h)	Tottenham H	W	1-0	Lyons	18,126
31		28	(h)	Wolves	W	3-0	Telfer 2, Hamilton	21,827
32	Mar	6	(a)	Leicester C	L	0-1		18,490
33		13	(h)	Q.P.R.	L	0-2		25,006
34		20	(h)	Leeds U	L	1-3	Lyons	28,556
35		27	(a)	Ipswich T	L	0-1		22,373
36	Apr	3	(a)	Liverpool	L	0-1		54,632
37		7	(h)	Stoke C	W	2-1	Hamilton, Bernard (pen)	16,974
38		10	(h)	Arsenal	D	0-0		20,774
39		17	(a)	Manchester U	L	1-2	Telfer	61,879
40		19	(h)	Middlesbrough	W	3-1	Pearson, Latchford, Connolly	18,204
41		21	(a)	Derby Co	W	3-1	King 2, Pearson	22,488
42		24	(h)	West Ham U	W	2-0	Bernard (pen), Pearson	26,101

FINAL LEAGUE POSITION: 11th in Division One

Appearances

Sub. Appearances

Goals

Lawson	Bernard	Seargeant	Clements	Kenyon	Hurst	Lyons	Dobson	Latchford	Smallman	Pearson	Marshall	Darracott	Buckley	Telfer	Jones G	Davies	McLaughlin	McNaught	Jones D	Irving	Brand	Hamilton	Goodlass	Connolly	Robinson	King	
1	2	3	4	5	6	7	8	9	10	11																	1
1	2	3	4	5		6	8	9	10	11	7																2
1			3	5	12	6	8	9	10	4	11*	2	7														3
1	2		3	5		6	8	9	10	4	11*		7	12													4
1	2		3	5		6	8	9	10	4	11*		7	12													5
1	2		3	5		6	8	9	10	4			7		11												6
1	2	3	12	5		6	8	9	10	4*			7		11												7
1	2	3		5		6	8	9	10	4			7		11												8
		3		5		6	8	9	10	4			7		11	1	2										9
	2	3		5		6	8	9		4*			7	10	11	1		12									10
	2	3	10	5		6	8	9		4			7		11	1											11
	2	3	10			6	8	9	12	4			7*		11	1		5									12
	2	3	5*			6	8	9	10	4			7		11	1		12									13
		3				6	8	9	10	4			7		11*	1	2	5	12								14
		3		11		6	8		10	4		2	7*	12		1		5		9							15
1		3				6	8		10	4		2	7	12	11			5		9*							16
1		3	4			6	8	9		12		2*	7	10	11			5									17
		3	4	5		6	8	9		12		2	7*		11						1	10					18
1	4	3		5		6	8	9		12		2		10	11							7*					19
	4	3*		5		6	8	9				2	12	10	11	1						7					20
	2			5		6	8	9				3	7	10	11	1						4					21
	2			5	12	6	8	9				3	7	10*	11	1						4					22
	2		5	4		6	8	9	10			3				1						7	11				23
	2		5	4		6	8	9	10			3*	11			1	12					7					24
	2		5	4		6	8	9	10			3	11*			1						7		12			25
1	2		5	4		6	8	9	10*			3			11							7					26
1	3		5	4		6	8	9						10	11							7			2		27
1	3			4		6	8	9				2		6	11			5				7		10			28
1	2		5*	4	6		8					3	11		12				9			7		10			29
1	2			4		6	8	9				3			11			5				7		10			30
1	2			4		6	8	9				3			11			5				7	10				31
1	2			4		6	8	9							11			5	3			7		10			32
1	2			4		6	8	9							11			5	3			7	12	10*			33
1	2	12		4		6	8	9							11*			5	3			7		10			34
1	2			4		6	8	9		11								5	3			7		10			35
	2		12	4		6	8	9					6		11	1		5*				7		10			36
	2			4	6		8	9							11	1		5	3			7		10			37
	2		12	4		6	8	9		6					11	1		5	3			7*		10			38
				4	6		8	9				2	7*		11	1		5	3			12		10			39
			5		12		8	9		11		2				1			3			7*		10		6	40
	12		5*	4			8	9		11		2				1						7	3	10		6	41
1	2			4			8	9		11			7									5	3	10		6	42
22	29	17	11	28	6	42	42	31	14	26	4	20	30	20	24	19	2	18	11	3	1	22	2	14	1	3	
		1	1	1	2	3				1	3		1	4	1			1	2	2		1	1	1			
	2	2		1		5	5	12	4	5		1	8	7								5		1		2	

17

1976-77

1	Aug	21	(a)	Q.P.R.	W	4-0	Parkes (og), Latchford 2, Bernard (pen)	24,449
2		24	(h)	Ipswich T	D	1-1	Telfer	33,070
3		28	(h)	Aston Villa	L	0-2		32,055
4	Sep	4	(a)	Leicester C	D	1-1	Latchford	18,083
5		11	(h)	Stoke C	W	3-0	Telfer 2, Latchford	22,277
6		18	(a)	Arsenal	L	1-3	Telfer	34,076
7		25	(h)	Bristol C	W	2-0	Dobson, Latchford	25,761
8	Oct	2	(a)	Sunderland	W	1-0	Goodlass	34,670
9		5	(h)	Manchester C	D	2-2	Dobson, King	31,370
10		16	(a)	Liverpool	L	1-3	Dobson	55,141
11		23	(h)	West Ham U	W	3-2	Lyons, King, Latchford	23,163
12		30	(a)	Tottenham H	D	3-3	King, McNaught, Latchford	26,047
13	Nov	6	(h)	Leeds U	L	0-2		32,618
14		20	(h)	Derby Co	W	2-0	King, Latchford	23,020
15		24	(a)	Newcastle U	L	1-4	Lyons	31,203
16		27	(a)	West Brom A	L	0-3		21,078
17	Dec	11	(a)	Coventry C	L	2-4	King, Kenyon	18,977
18		18	(h)	Birmingham C	D	2-2	McKenzie 2 (1 pen)	32,532
19		27	(a)	Manchester U	L	0-4		56,786
20		29	(h)	Middlesbrough	D	2-2	McNaught, Latchford	28,169
21	Jan	15	(a)	Ipswich T	L	0-2		25,570
22		22	(h)	Q.P.R.	L	1-3	McKenzie	26,875
23	Feb	5	(a)	Aston Villa	L	0-2		41,305
24		12	(h)	Leicester C	L	1-2	Latchford	28,024
25		19	(a)	Stoke C	W	1-0	Dobson	19,543
26	Mar	1	(h)	Arsenal	W	2-1	Latchford, Jones	29,902
27		5	(a)	Bristol C	W	2-1	Latchford, Gillies (og)	21,108
28		22	(h)	Liverpool	D	0-0		56,562
29		26	(h)	Tottenham H	W	4-0	Latchford, King (pen), Dobson, Lyons	32,549
30	Apr	2	(a)	West Ham U	D	2-2	Goodlass, Pearson	22,518
31		5	(h)	Manchester U	L	1-2	Dobson	38,216
32		9	(a)	Middlesbrough	D	2-2	Pearson, Latchford	16,159
33		16	(a)	Derby Co	W	3-2	Latchford, Pejic, McKenzie	23,443
34		19	(h)	Norwich C	W	3-1	McNaught, King, Pearson	28,856
35		30	(a)	Norwich C	L	1-2	Pearson	19,091
36	May	4	(a)	Leeds U	D	0-0		22,175
37		7	(h)	Coventry C	D	1-1	Rioch	24,569
38		10	(a)	Manchester C	D	1-1	Lyons	38,004
39		14	(a)	Birmingham C	D	1-1	Latchford	22,660
40		16	(h)	West Brom A	D	1-1	Dobson	20,102
41		19	(h)	Sunderland	W	2-0	Latchford, Rioch	36,075
42		24	(h)	Newcastle U	W	2-0	Dobson, McKenzie	25,208

FINAL LEAGUE POSITION: 9th in Division One

Appearances

Sub. Appearances

Goals

Davies	Bernard	Jones	Lyons	Kenyon	McNaught	King	Dobson	Latchford	Pearson	Telfer	Seargeant	Smallman	Goodlass	Darracott	Hamilton	Higgins	Buckley	Rioch	McKenzie	Lawson	Pejic	Robinson	Brand	No.
1	2	3	4	5	6	7	8	9	10	11														1
1	2		4	6	5	7	8	9	10	11	3													2
1	2	3	4	6	5	7	8	9	10*	11		12												3
1	2	3	4	6	5	7	8	9		11			10											4
1	2	3	4	6	5	7	8	9		11			10											5
1	2*	3	4	6	5	7	8	9		11			10	12										6
1		3	4		5	7	8	9		11			10	2	6									7
1		3	4		5	7	8	9		11			10	2	6									8
1	2		4		5	7	8	9		11			10		6	3								9
1	6*	3	4		5	7	8	9	12	11			10	2										10
1		3	4		5	7	8*	9	12	11			10	2	6									11
1	2	3	4		5	7	8	9		11*			10	12	6									12
1	2	3	4	6	5	7	8	9				11*	10				12							13
1	2	3	4	6	5	7	8	9		11			10											14
1	2	3	4	6	5	7*	8	9		11			10	12										15
1		3	4*	6	5	7	8	9		12			10	2	11									16
1		3		6	5	7	8	9					11	2				4	10					17
		3	4		5	7	8	9					11	2				6	10	1				18
		3	4		5	7	8	9					11	2				6	10	1				19
	2		4		5	7	8	9			3		11					6	10	1				20
	2		4		5	7	8	9			3			11				6	10	1				21
		3	4		5	7	8	9					11	2*			12	6	10	1				22
	2	3	4		5	7	8	9					11					6	10	1				23
	2	3	4		5	7*	8	9					12		11			6	10	1				24
		2	6		5		8	9					11		7			4	10	1	3			25
		2	4		5		8	9					11		7			6	10	1	3			26
		2	4	5	6		8	9					11		7				10	1	3			27
			4	7*	5	6	8	9	11	12				2				10		1	3			28
			4		5	6	8	9					11	2				10	7	1	3			29
		2	4		5		8	9	12	10*			11	6	7					1	3			30
	3*		4	7	5	6	8	9	10				11	2			12			1				31
	12		4*	5	6		8	9	10				11	2				7		1	3			32
1			4		5		8	9*					11		7		12	6	10		3	2		33
1			4		5	6*	8		10				11				12	7	9		3	2		34
1			4		5		8	9					11*	2	12		7	6	10		3			35
1			4		5	11		9						2	8		7	6	10		3			36
1			4		5	11	8	9						2	7			6	10		3			37
1			4		5	12	8	9					11*	2	7			6	10		3			38
1	12		4		5	11	8	9	10*					2				7	6		3			39
1	6		4		5	11	8	9	10*				12	2				7			3			40
1			4		5		8	9					11		7			6	10		3	2		41
					5	7	8	9*	12				11			4		6	10		3	2	1	42
26	14	28	39	14	42	36	40	36	12	17	4	1	29	20	16	2	7	22	20	15	17	4	1	
	1		1		1				4	2		1	2	3	2		4							
	1	1	4	1	3	7	8	17	4	4			2					2	5		1			

1977-78

1	Aug	20	(h)	Nottingham F	L 1-3	Pearson	38,001
2		23	(a)	Arsenal	L 0-1		32,954
3		27	(a)	Aston Villa	W 2-1	McKenzie 2	37,806
4	Sep	3	(h)	Wolves	D 0-0		36,636
5		10	(a)	Leicester C	W 5-1	Latchford, Thomas, King 2, McKenzie	16,425
6		17	(h)	Norwich C	W 3-0	Rioch, McKenzie, Dobson	34,405
7		24	(a)	West Ham U	D 1-1	McKenzie	25,296
8	Oct	1	(h)	Manchester C	D 1-1	Latchford	43,286
9		4	(h)	West Brom A	W 3-1	Higgins, King (pen), Latchford	34,582
10		8	(a)	Q.P.R.	W 5-1	Latchford 4, McKenzie	20,495
11		15	(h)	Bristol C	W 1-0	King	39,230
12		22	(a)	Liverpool	D 0-0		51,668
13		29	(h)	Newcastle U	D 4-4	Pejic, Latchford 2, Lyons	37,647
14	Nov	5	(a)	Derby C	W 1-0	Lyons	29,335
15		12	(h)	Birmingham C	W 2-1	Latchford 2	37,743
16		19	(a)	Ipswich T	D 3-3	Lyons, Pearson, Buckley	22,790
17		26	(h)	Coventry C	W 6-0	Dobson, Latchford 3, Pearson, King	43,309
18	Dec	3	(a)	Chelsea	W 1-0	Latchford	33,890
19		10	(h)	Middlesbrough	W 3-0	Latchford 2, Buckley	38,647
20		17	(a)	Birmingham C	D 0-0		22,177
21		26	(h)	Manchester U	L 2-6	Latchford, Dobson	48,335
22		27	(a)	Leeds U	L 1-3	Dobson	46,727
23		31	(h)	Arsenal	W 2-0	Latchford, King	47,035
24	Jan	2	(a)	Nottingham F	D 1-1	Ross (pen)	44,030
25		14	(h)	Aston Villa	W 1-0	King	40,630
26		21	(a)	Wolves	L 1-3	Ross (pen)	23,777
27	Feb	4	(h)	Leicester C	W 2-0	Latchford 2	33,707
28		18	(h)	West Ham U	W 2-1	McKenzie, Thomas	33,826
29		25	(a)	Manchester C	L 0-1		46,817
30	Mar	4	(h)	Q.P.R.	D 3-3	Ross, Dobson, King	33,861
31		11	(a)	Bristol C	W 1-0	Ross	25,614
32		15	(a)	Norwich C	D 0-0		18,905
33		24	(a)	Newcastle U	W 2-0	Latchford, McKenzie	28,933
34		25	(h)	Leeds U	W 2-0	Latchford, McKenzie	45,020
35		27	(a)	Manchester U	W 2-1	Latchford 2	55,277
36	Apr	1	(h)	Derby Co	W 2-1	Dobson, Latchford	38,213
37		5	(h)	Liverpool	L 0-1		52,759
38		8	(a)	Coventry C	L 2-3	Latchford, Lyons	26,008
39		15	(h)	Ipswich T	W 1-0	Latchford (pen)	33,402
40		22	(a)	Middlesbrough	D 0-0		15,969
41		25	(a)	West Brom A	L 1-3	Telfer	20,247
42		29	(h)	Chelsea	W 6-0	Dobson, Wright, Robinson, Lyons, Latchford 2 (1 pen)	39,500

FINAL LEAGUE POSITION: 3rd in Division One

Appearances

Sub. Appearances

Goals

Wood	Jones	Pejic	Lyons	Kenyon	Higgins	King	Darracott	Pearson	McKenzie	Thomas	Goodlass	Latchford	Rioch	Dobson	Telfer	Buckley	Ross	Seargeant	Wright	Robinson	No.
1	2	3	4	5	6	7	8*	9	10	11	12										1
1		3	4	5*	12	7	2	8	10	11		9	6								2
1		3	4		5	7	2	8	10	11		9	6								3
1		3	4		5	7	2	8	10	11		9		6							4
1	12	3	4		5	7	2*		10	11		9	6	8							5
1	12	3	4		5	7	2		10	11		9	6*	8							6
1	12	3	4		5	7	2		10	11*		9	6	8							7
1		3	4		5	7	2		10	11		9	6	8							8
1	2	3	4		5	7		6	10	11		9		8							9
1	2	3	4		5	7		6	10	11		9		8							10
1	2	3	4		5	7	12	10				9		8	11	6*					11
1	2	3	4		5	7		10		11		9	6	8							12
1	2	3	4		5	7		10		11		9*	6	8	12						13
1	2*		4		5	7		10		11		9		8		6	3	12			14
1	2	3	4		5	7		10		11		9		8		6					15
1	2	3*	4		5	7		10		11		9		8		6	12				16
1	2	3	4		5	7		10		11		9		8		6					17
1	2	3	4		5	7		10		11		9		8		6					18
1	2	3	4		5	7		10		11		9		8		6					19
1	2	3	4		5	7		10		11		9		8		6					20
1	2	3	4		5	7		10*		11		9		8		6	12				21
1	2	3	4		5	7			10	11		9		8			6				22
1		3	4	5		7	2		10	11		9		8			6				23
1	12	3	4	5*		7	2		10	11		9		8			6				24
1		3	4		5	7	2		10	11		9		8			6				25
1	12	3	4	5		7	2*	8	10	11		9					6				26
1	2	3	4		5	7			10			9		8	11*		6		12		27
1	2	3	4		5	7			10	11		9*		8	12		6				28
1	2	3	4		5	7		9	10					8	11		6				29
1	2*	3	4	5		7		9	10	11				8	12		6				30
1	2	3	4	5		7			10	11		9		8			6				31
1	2	3	4			7	5		10	11		9		8			6				32
1	2	3	4			7	2	12	10*			9		8	11		6				33
1	2	3	4			7	5		10	11		9		8			6				34
1	2	3	4			7	5		10	11		9		8			6				35
1	2	3	4			7	5		10	11		9		8			6				36
1	2	3	4			7	5		10	11		9		8			6				37
1	2	3	4			7	5		10	11		9		8			6				38
1	2	3	4			7			10	11		9		8		6			5		39
1	2		4			7		6		11		9		8	10				5	2	40
1		3	4			7				11		9		8	10	6			5	2	41
1		3	4			7				11		9		8	10	6			5	2	42
42	29	40	42	7	25	42	19	21	28	38		39	8	38	7	12	18		3	4	
	5			1		1	1				1		3			2	1	1			
		1	5		1	8		3	9	2		30	1	7	1	2	4		1	1	

21

1978-79

1	Aug	19	(a)	Chelsea	W	1-0	King	32,683
2		22	(h)	Derby Co	W	2-1	King, Nulty	40,125
3		26	(h)	Arsenal	W	1-0	Thomas	41,161
4	Sep	2	(a)	Manchester U	D	1-1	King	53,982
5		9	(h)	Middlesbrough	W	2-0	Lyons, Dobson	36,191
6		16	(a)	Aston Villa	D	1-1	Walsh	39,636
7		23	(h)	Wolves	W	2-0	Latchford, King (pen)	38,895
8		30	(a)	Bristol C	D	2-2	Latchford 2	22,502
9	Oct	7	(h)	Southampton	D	0-0		38,769
10		14	(a)	Ipswich T	W	1-0	Latchford	22,830
11		21	(a)	Q.P.R.	D	1-1	Latchford	21,171
12		28	(h)	Liverpool	W	1-0	King	53,141
13	Nov	4	(a)	Nottingham F	D	0-0		35,515
14		11	(h)	Chelsea	W	3-2	King, Dobson 2	38,346
15		18	(a)	Arsenal	D	2-2	Ross, Dobson	39,711
16		21	(h)	Manchester U	W	3-0	Ross, King, Latchford	42,126
17		25	(a)	Norwich C	W	1-0	Lyons	18,930
18	Dec	9	(a)	Birmingham C	W	3-1	Ross (pen), Todd, Latchford	23,391
19		16	(h)	Leeds U	D	1-1	Ross	37,997
20		23	(a)	Coventry C	L	2-3	Lyons, Latchford	22,778
21		26	(h)	Manchester C	W	1-0	Wright	46,996
22		30	(h)	Tottenham H	D	1-1	Lyons	44,572
23	Jan	31	(a)	Aston Villa	D	1-1	Thomas	29,079
24	Feb	3	(a)	Wolves	L	0-1		21,892
25		10	(h)	Bristol C	W	4-1	King 3, Wright	29,116
26		17	(a)	Southampton	L	0-3		20,681
27		24	(h)	Ipswich T	L	0-1		29,031
28	Mar	3	(h)	Q.P.R.	W	2-1	Latchford, Telfer	24,809
29		6	(a)	Middlesbrough	W	2-1	Jack, Latchford	16,084
30		10	(h)	Nottingham F	D	1-1	Telfer	37,745
31		13	(a)	Liverpool	D	1-1	King	52,352
32		24	(a)	Derby Co	D	0-0		20,814
33		30	(h)	Norwich C	D	2-2	Lyons 2	26,825
34	Apr	3	(a)	Bolton W	L	1-3	Ross (pen)	27,263
35		7	(a)	West Brom A	L	0-1		29,593
36		10	(h)	Coventry C	D	3-3	Ross, Latchford, Kidd	25,302
37		14	(a)	Manchester C	D	0-0		39,711
38		16	(h)	Bolton W	W	1-0	Higgins	31,214
39		21	(a)	Leeds U	L	0-1		29,125
40		28	(h)	Birmingham C	W	1-0	King	23,048
41	May	1	(h)	West Brom A	L	0-2		30,083
42		5	(a)	Tottenham H	D	1-1	Kidd	26,077

FINAL LEAGUE POSITION : 4th in Division One

Appearances

Sub. Appearances

Goals

Wood	Darracott	Pejic	Lyons	Higgins	Nutty	King	Dobson	Latchford	Walsh	Thomas	Wright	Todd	Ross	Robinson	Kenyon	Jones	Telfer	Heard	Jack	Barton	Kidd	Eastoe	No.
1	2	3	4	5	6	7	8	9	10	11													1
1	2	3	4		6	7	8	9	10	11	5												2
1	2	3	4		6	7	8	9	10	11	5												3
1	2	3	4		6	7	8	9	10	11	5												4
1	2	3	4		6	7	8	9	10	11	5												5
1	2	3	4		6	7	8	9	10	11	5												6
1		3	4			7	8	9	10	11	5	2	6										7
1		3	4			7	8	9	10	11	5	2	6										8
1		3	4			7	8	9	10	11	5	2	6										9
1		3	4			7	8	9	10	11	5	2	6										10
1		3	4*		6	7	8	9	10	11	5	2		12									11
1		3			6	7	8	9	10	11	5	2			4								12
1	2	3				7	8	9	10	11	5	4	6										13
1		3	4			7	8	9	10*	11	5	2	6	12									14
1		3	4	12		7	8	9	10	11	5*	2	6										15
1		3	4	12		7	8	9	10*	11	5	2	6										16
1		3	4			7	8	9		11	5	2	6		10								17
1		3	4	10		7	8	9		11	5	2	6										18
1		3	4	10	12	7	8*	9		11	5	2	6										19
1			4	10	6	7	8	9		11	5	2				3							20
1			4	10	6	7	8	9			5	2		12		3*	11						21
1			4		6	7	8	9			5	2		10		3	11						22
1			4	3		7	8	9	10	11	5	2	6										23
1			4	3		7	8	9	10*	11	5	2	6				12						24
1			4	3		10	8	9		11	5	7	6					2					25
1			4	3		10	8	9		11	5	7	2					6					26
1			4	3		7	8	9	12	11*	5	2					10	6					27
1			4			7	8*	9	12	11	5	2	6				10	3					28
1			4	2			8	9		11	5		6				10	3	7				29
1			4	2		7	8	9	12	11	5		6				10*	3					30
1			4			7	8	9		11	5	2	6				10	3					31
1			4	9		7	8			11	5	2	6				10	3					32
1			4	9*		7	8			11	5	2	6				10	3		12			33
1			4	9			8			11		2	6		3	10				5	7		34
1			4			7	8	9		11*		2	6			3				2	10	12	35
1			4			7	8	9*			5		6			3	12			2	10	11	36
1			4				8	9			5	7	6		3*		12			2	10	11	37
1			4	5		7	8	9					6				3			2	10	11	38
1			4	5		7		9					6				3	8		2	10	11	39
1				5	12	7	8	9				4	6				3			2	10	11*	40
1			4	5		7	8	9					6				3			2	10	11	41
1				5		7	8	9				4	6				3			2	10	11	42
42	7	19	37	20	13	40	40	36	18	33	39	29	26	4	3	11	10	9	1	9	9	7	
				4					3				3				2	1		1		1	
		6	1	1		12	4	11	1	2	2	1	6				2		1	2			

23

1979-80

1	Aug	18	(h)	Norwich C	L	2-4	Ross (pen), Nulty	27,555
2		22	(a)	Leeds U	L	0-2		27,783
3		25	(a)	Derby Co	W	1-0	King	17,820
4	Sep	1	(h)	Aston Villa	D	1-1	Bailey	29,271
5		8	(a)	Stoke C	W	3-2	King, Bailey, Irvine (og)	23,460
6		15	(h)	Wolves	L	2-3	Kidd, Ross (pen)	31,807
7		22	(a)	Ipswich T	D	1-1	Kidd	19,279
8		29	(h)	Bristol C	D	0-0		24,733
9	Oct	6	(a)	Coventry C	L	1-2	King	17,205
10		13	(h)	Crystal Palace	W	3-1	Kidd, Latchford, King	30,645
11		20	(a)	Liverpool	D	2-2	Kidd, King	52,201
12		27	(h)	Manchester U	D	0-0		37,708
13	Nov	3	(a)	Norwich C	D	0-0		18,025
14		10	(h)	Middlesbrough	L	0-2		25,155
15		13	(h)	Leeds U	W	5-1	Latchford 3, Kidd, Hart (og)	23,319
16		17	(a)	Arsenal	L	0-2		33,450
17		24	(h)	Tottenham H	D	1-1	Latchford	31,079
18	Dec	1	(a)	West Brom A	D	1-1	King	21,237
19		8	(h)	Brighton & H.A.	W	2-0	King, Kidd	23,595
20		15	(a)	Southampton	L	0-1		19,850
21		22	(h)	Manchester C	L	1-2	Kidd	26,314
22		26	(a)	Bolton W	D	1-1	McBride	18,220
23		29	(h)	Derby Co	D	1-1	King	22,554
24	Jan	1	(h)	Nottingham F	W	1-0	Kidd	34,622
25		12	(a)	Aston Villa	L	1-2	Eastoe	22,635
26	Feb	2	(a)	Wolves	L	0-0		21,663
27		9	(h)	Ipswich T	L	0-4		31,603
28		19	(a)	Bristol C	L	1-2	Ross	16,317
29		23	(a)	Crystal Palace	D	1-1	Eastoe	23,400
30	Mar	1	(h)	Liverpool	L	1-2	Eastoe	53,018
31		12	(a)	Manchester U	D	0-0		45,515
32		15	(h)	Coventry C	D	1-1	Eastoe	25,970
33		18	(h)	Stoke C	W	2-0	Latchford, Eastoe	23,847
34		22	(a)	Middlesbrough	L	1-2	Hartford	17,587
35		28	(h)	Arsenal	L	0-1		28,184
36	Apr	2	(a)	Manchester C	D	1-1	King	33,437
37		5	(h)	Bolton W	W	3-1	Megson, Eastoe, Kidd	28,037
38		19	(a)	Tottenham H	L	0-3		25,245
39		26	(h)	Southampton	W	2-0	Stanley, Gidman (pen)	23,552
40		28	(h)	West Brom A	D	0-0		20,356
41	May	3	(a)	Brighton & H.A.	D	0-0		21,204
42		9	(a)	Nottingham F	L	0-1		22,122

FINAL LEAGUE POSITION: 19th in Division One

Appearances

Sub. Appearances

Goals

Wood	Barton	Bailey	Lyons	Wright	Ross	Nulty	Todd	King	Kidd	Heard	Eastoe	Higgins	Hartford	Stanley	Latchford	Varadi	Gidman	Hodge	O'Keefe	McBridge	Megson	Ratcliffe	Sharp	
1	2	3	4	5	6	7	8	9	10	11*	12													1
1	2	3	4	11	6	7	8	9	10			5												2
1	2	3	4	11	6	7	8	9	10			5												3
1		3	4	2	6			9	10		11	5	7	8										4
1		3	4	2	6			9	10		11	5	7	8										5
1	12	3	4	2	6			9	10		11*	5	7	8										6
1	2	3	4	8	6	9			10		11	5	7											7
1	2*	3	4	12	6			9	10		11	5	7	8										8
1	2	3	4		6			11	10			5	7	8	9*	12								9
1		3	4	2	6	12		11	10			5	7*	8	9									10
1		3	4	2	6	7		11	10			5		8	9									11
1		3	4	8	6	7			10		11	5			9		2							12
1		3	4	8	6			11	10			5	7		9		2							13
1		3	12	4	6			11	10			5	7*	8	9		2							14
		3	12	4	6			11	10			5	7	8	9*		2	1						15
		3	12	4	6			11	10			5	7	8	9*		2	1						16
		3		4	6			11	10			5	7	8	9		2	1						17
		3		4	6			11	10			5	7	8	9		2	1						18
		3		4	6			11	10			5	7	8	9		2	1						19
		3		4	6			11	10		12	5	7	8	9*	10	2	1						20
		3	5	4	6			11	10				7	8*	9	12	2	1						21
		3	5	4					10				7	8	9		2	1	6	11				22
		3	5	4	6				10				7	8	9		2	1		11				23
		3	5	4	6				10				7	8	9		2	1		11				24
		3	5	4	6*				10		8		7		9		2	1	12	11				25
		3	5	4				8	10		6				9		2	1		11	7			26
		3	5	4				8	10		6				9		2	1	6	11	7			27
		3	5	4	6				10		8				9		2	1		11	7			28
		3	5	2	6	4			10		8				9			1		11	7			29
1		3	5	8	6	4*		9	10		12		7				2			11				30
		3	5	2				8	10		6				9			1		11	7	4		31
		3	5	4	8			6	10				9				2	1		11	7			32
		3	5	4	8			6	10				9				2	1		11	7			33
		3	5	4	8			6	10				9				2	1		11	7			34
		3	5	4	12			6	10		8		9				2	1		11	7*			35
		3	5	4	11			8	9		6		10				2	1			7			36
		3	5	4	11			8	9		6		10				2	1			7			37
		3*	5	2	11			9	8		10			4				1	12	7	6			38
1		3	5	4	6			7	10				8	9			2			11				39
1		3	5	4	6			7	10				8	9			2			11				40
1		3	5	4	6			7	10				8	9*			2			11			12	41
1		3	5	4	6			7	10				8				2		11			9		42
19	6	42	35	40	31	9	3	29	31	1	23	19	35	24	26	2	29	23	3	17	12	2	1	
	1			3	1	1	1				3					2			1	1		1		
		2		3	1			9	9		6		1	1	6		1			1	1			

25

1980-81

1	Aug	16	(a)	Sunderland	L	1-3	Eastoe	32,005
2		19	(h)	Leicester C	W	1-0	Eastoe	23,337
3		23	(h)	Nottingham F	D	0-0		25,981
4		30	(a)	Ipswich T	L	0-4		20,879
5	Sep	6	(h)	Wolves	W	2-0	Eastoe, Wright	21,820
6		13	(a)	Aston Villa	W	2-0	Lyons, Eastoe	25,673
7		20	(h)	Crystal Palace	W	5-0	Latchford 3, Gidman (pen), Eastoe	26,950
8		27	(a)	Coventry C	W	5-0	Eastoe, Latchford 2, McBride 2	14,810
9	Oct	4	(h)	Southampton	W	2-1	McBride 2 (2 pens)	36,544
10		7	(a)	Brighton & H.A.	W	3-1	McMahon, Lyons, McBride	16,523
11		11	(a)	Leeds U	L	0-1		25,601
12		18	(h)	Liverpool	D	2-2	Hartford, McBride	52,565
13		21	(h)	West Brom A	D	1-1	Eastoe	24,046
14		25	(a)	Manchester U	L	0-2		54,260
15	Nov	1	(h)	Tottenham H	D	2-2	Eastoe, McMahon	26,174
16		8	(a)	Norwich C	L	1-2	Latchford	14,557
17		12	(a)	Leicester C	W	1-0	Eastoe	15,511
18		15	(h)	Sunderland	W	2-1	O'Keefe, Hartford	24,099
19		22	(a)	Arsenal	L	1-2	Wright	30,911
20		29	(h)	Birmingham C	D	1-1	O'Keefe	22,258
21	Dec	6	(a)	Stoke C	D	2-2	McBride, Varadi	15,650
22		13	(h)	Brighton & H.A.	W	4-3	Eastoe 2, McMahon, Varadi	19,157
23		26	(h)	Manchester C	L	0-2		36,194
24		27	(a)	Middlesbrough	L	0-1		20,210
25	Jan	10	(h)	Arsenal	L	1-2	O'Keefe	29,360
26		17	(h)	Ipswich T	D	0-0		25,516
27		31	(a)	Nottingham F	L	0-1		25,611
28	Feb	7	(h)	Aston Villa	L	1-3	Ross (pen)	31,434
29		21	(h)	Coventry C	W	3-0	Ross, McMahon, Eastoe	26,731
30		28	(a)	Crystal Palace	W	3-2	Eastoe, McMahon, Varadi	14,594
31	Mar	14	(h)	Leeds U	L	1-2	Varadi	23,014
32		17	(a)	Southampton	L	0-3		20,829
33		21	(a)	Liverpool	L	0-1		49,743
34		28	(h)	Manchester U	L	0-1		25,854
35		31	(a)	West Brom A	L	0-2		14,833
36	Apr	4	(a)	Tottenham H	D	2-2	Hartford, Varadi	27,208
37		11	(h)	Norwich C	L	0-2		16,254
38		18	(h)	Middlesbrough	W	4-1	Hartford 2 (1 pen), Megson, Eastoe	15,706
39		20	(a)	Manchester C	L	1-3	Varadi	34,434
40		25	(h)	Stoke C	L	0-1		15,352
41	May	2	(a)	Birmingham C	D	1-1	Eastoe	12,863
42		4	(a)	Wolves	D	0-0		16,269

FINAL LEAGUE POSITION: 15th in Division One

Appearances

Sub. Appearances

Goals

26

McDonagh	Gidman	Ratcliffe	Wright	Lyons	Megson	McMahon	Sharp	Latchford	Hartford	McBride	Eastoe	Stanley	O'Keefe	Bailey	Ross	Higgins	Varadi	Hodge	Lodge	Telfer	Barton	
1	2	3	4	5	6*	7	8	9	10	11	12											1
1	2	3	4	5		7		9	10	11	8	6										2
1	2	3	4	5		7		9	10	11	8	6										3
1	2	3	4	5		7		9	8	11	10	6*	12									4
1	2		4	5		7		9*	10	11	8	6	12	3								5
1	2		4	5		7		9	1	11	8*	6	12	3								6
1	2		4	5		7		9	10	11	8	6		3								7
1	2		4	5		7		9	10*	11	8	6	12	3								8
1	2		4	5	10	7		9		11	8	6		3	2							9
1	2		4	5		7		9	10	11	8*	6	12	3								10
1	2		4	5		7		9	10	11	8	6*	12	3								11
1	2*		4	5		7		9	10	11	8	6	12	3								12
1			4	5		7		9	10	11	8	6		3								13
1	2		4	5		7		9	10	11	8	6*	12	3								14
1	2		4	5		7		9*	10	11	8	6	12	3								15
1	2		4	5*		7		9	10	11	8	6	12	3								16
1	2		4			7		9	10	11	8	5	6	3								17
1	2		4		12	7		9*	10	11	8	5	6	3								18
1	2		4		6	7			10	11	8	5	9	3								19
1	2		4		6	7			10	11	8	5	9	3								20
1		2				7			10	11	8	4	6	3	5		9					21
1		2	12			7			10	11	8	4	6*	3	5		9					22
1	2	5	4	12		7			10	11*	8		6	3			9					23
1	2	5	4	12		7			10	11	8			3	6		9*					24
1	2	5	4			7			10		8		11	3	6		9					25
1		2	4	5		7			10	12	8		11*	3	6		9					26
		2	4	5		7			10	12	8		11*	3	6		9	1				27
		2	4	5		7			10		8		11*	3	6		9	1	12			28
1	2*	3	4	5		7			10		8		11		6		9		12			29
1	2	3	4	5		7			10		8		11		6*		9		12			30
1	2		4	5		7			10	11	8		3		6		9					31
1	2	3	4	5*		7			10	12	8	6			11		9					32
1	2		4			7				12	8	5	11	3	6		9*		10			33
1	2	12	4			7					8	5	11	3*	6		9		10			34
1	2	3	4			7*			10		8	5			6	12	11		9			35
1	2		4	6					10		8	5	3		7		9*		11	12		36
1	2	3	4	5	12				10		8*	6			7		9		11			37
1	2	3	4	5		7		12	10		8	6*					9		11			38
1	2	3	4	5		7		12	10	11	8*						9		6			39
1		4		5		7		9	10	11*	8		3				12		6		2	40
1	6	4	7	5					10		8		3			11	9				2	41
1	6	4	7	5				12	10		8*		3		11		9				2	42
40	35	20	41	30	8	34	2	18	39	27	41	28	15	31	17	2	20	2	8	1	3	
		1		3	2		2	1		4	1		10				2		3	1		
	1		2	2	1	5		6	5	7	15		3		2		6					

1981-82

1	Aug	29	(h)	Birmingham C	W	3-1	Ainscow, Eastoe, Biley	33,045
2	Sep	2	(a)	Leeds U	D	1-1	Biley	26,502
3		5	(a)	Southampton	L	0-1		21,624
4		12	(h)	Brighton & H.A.	D	1-1	Wright	27,352
5		19	(a)	Tottenham H	L	0-3		31,219
6		22	(h)	Notts Co	W	3-1	Eastoe, Ross, O'Keefe	22,175
7		26	(h)	West Brom A	W	1-0	Lyons	23,873
8	Oct	3	(a)	Stoke C	L	1-3	McBride	16,007
9		10	(a)	West Ham U	D	1-1	McMahon	31,608
10		17	(h)	Ipswich T	W	2-1	Ferguson, Stevens	25,146
11		24	(a)	Middlesbrough	W	2-0	Ferguson 2	13,423
12		31	(h)	Manchester C	L	0-1		31,305
13	Nov	7	(a)	Liverpool	L	1-3	Ferguson	48,861
14		21	(h)	Sunderland	L	1-2	Eastoe	19,759
15		24	(a)	Notts Co	D	2-2	Biley, Sharp	7,771
16		28	(a)	Arsenal	L	0-1		25,860
17	Dec	5	(h)	Swansea C	W	3-1	Sharp, O'Keefe 2	23,860
18		19	(h)	Aston Villa	W	2-0	Lyons, Eastoe	16,538
19		28	(h)	Coventry C	W	3-2	Higgins 2, Sharp	23,895
20	Jan	6	(a)	Manchester U	D	1-1	Sharp	40,451
21		19	(h)	Southampton	D	1-1	Richardson	22,355
22		23	(a)	Wolves	W	3-0	Richardson, Irvine 2	11,784
23		30	(h)	Tottenham H	D	1-1	Sharp	30,717
24	Feb	6	(a)	Brighton & H.A.	L	1-3	Heath	16,148
25		13	(h)	Stoke C	D	0-0		20,656
26		20	(a)	West Brom A	D	0-0		14,819
27		27	(h)	West Ham U	D	0-0		28,618
28	Mar	6	(a)	Ipswich T	L	0-3		19,360
29		13	(h)	Middlesbrough	W	2-0	Higgins, Sharp	15,807
30		20	(a)	Manchester C	D	1-1	Heath	33,002
31		27	(h)	Liverpool	L	1-3	Sharp	51,847
32	Apr	3	(a)	Nottingham F	W	1-0	McMahon	17,323
33		6	(a)	Birmingham C	W	2-0	Heath, Ainscow	12,273
34		10	(h)	Manchester U	D	3-3	Sharp, Lyons, Heath	29,317
35		13	(a)	Coventry C	L	0-1		11,858
36		17	(a)	Sunderland	L	1-3	Irvine	18,359
37		20	(h)	Nottingham F	W	2-1	Sharp 2	15,460
38		24	(h)	Arsenal	W	2-1	Wright, Heath	19,136
39	May	1	(a)	Swansea C	W	3-1	Heath, Sharp 2 (1 pen)	16,243
40		4	(h)	Leeds U	W	1-0	Sharp	17,137
41		8	(h)	Wolves	D	1-1	Eastoe	20,124
42		15	(a)	Aston Villa	W	2-1	Sharp 2	20,446

FINAL LEAGUE POSITION: 8th in Division One

Appearances

Sub. Appearances

Goals

Arnold	Wright	Bailey	Walsh	Lyons	Thomas	Ainscow	Eastoe	Biley	Hartford	Ross	Ratcliffe	McMahon	Ferguson	O'Keefe	McBride	Sharp	Stevens	Higgins	Southall	Lodge	Richardson	Kendall	Irvine	Heath	Borrows	Rimmer	
1	2	3	4	5	6	7	8	9	10	11																	1
1	2		4	5	6	11	8	9	10		3	7															2
1	2		4	5	6	11	8	9	10		3	7*	12														3
1	2		4	5	6	11	8	9	10		3	7															4
1	2		4	5	6	11	8	9	10		3	7*		12													5
1	2		4	5	6	11	8	9*	10	7	3			12													6
1	2		4	5	6			9	10	7	3	8*		11	12												7
1	2	3*	4	5	6			9	10	7		8		11	12												8
1		3		5	6		8*		10	7		9	12	11			2	4									9
		3	4	5	6*			12	10	7		9	8	11			2		1								10
1		3		5		10*		12		7		9	8	11			2	4			6						11
1		3		5		10*				7		9	8	11	12		2	4			6						12
1		3		5		10*		12		7		9	8	11			2	4			6						13
1		3	4	5		10	8*	9		7				11			2				6	12					14
1			4	5		11*		10			3	7				9	2				6	12	8				15
1			4	5				10		8	3	7		11		9	2				6						16
1			4	5				10		8	3	7		11		9	2						6				17
				5			10			8	3					9	2	4	1	11		6	7				18
				5			10			8	3	7				9	2	4	1			6	11				19
				5			10			8	3	7				9	2	4	1	11			6				20
				5			10				3					9	2	4	1	11	6		7	8			21
				5			10				3					9	2	4	1	11	6		7	8			22
				5			10				3					9	2	4	1	11	6		7	8			23
				5			10				3					9	2	4	1	11	6		7	8			24
	5									11	3	10				9		4	1		6		7	8	2		25
	5						10			11	3					9		4	1		6		7	8	2		26
	5						10			11	3					9		4	1		6		7	8	2		27
	5						10*			11	3	12				9		4	1		6		7	8	2		28
	5							12		11	3	10*				9		4	1		6		7	8	2		29
	5									11	3	10				9		4	1		6		7	8	2		30
	5									11	3	10				9		4	1		6		7	8	2		31
	5						12	10		11	3	6				9*		4	1				7	8	2		32
	5*						10	12		11	3	6				9		4	1				7	8	2		33
			5				10			11	3	6				9		4	1*	12			7	8	2		34
			5				10			11	3	6				9		4	1				7	8	2		35
	5					12	10				3	6	9					4	1		11		7*	8	2		36
	5									11	3	6				9		4	1		10		7	8	2		37
	5	3								11		6				9	2	4	1		10		7	8			38
	5	3								11		6				9	2	4	1		12		7	8		10*	39
	5	3						12		11		6				9	2	4	1				7	8		10*	40
	5	3					10			11		6				9		4	1				7	8	2		41
	5	3					10			11		6				9		4	1				7	8	2		42
16	24	12	18	26	10	15	17	16	7	27	25	31	7	8	7	27	19	29	26	12	15	4	25	22	15	2	
			1		2	2	3				1	1	3	1	2					1	3						
	2		3		2	5	3		1		2	4	3	1	15	1	3				2		3	6			

1982-83

1	Aug	28	(a)	Watford	L	0-2		19,630
2		31	(h)	Aston Villa	W	5-0	Heath 2, King, Sharp 2 (1 pen)	24,026
3	Sep	4	(h)	Tottenham H	W	3-1	Sheedy, Wright, McMahon	30,553
4		8	(a)	Manchester U	L	1-2	King	43,186
5		11	(a)	Notts Co	L	0-1		9,197
6		18	(h)	Norwich C	D	1-1	Irvine	20,281
7		25	(a)	Coventry C	L	2-4	Heath, King	9,319
8	Oct	2	(h)	Brighton & H.A.	D	2-2	Heath, Wright	17,539
9		9	(h)	Manchester C	W	2-1	King, McMahon	25,158
10		16	(a)	Swansea C	W	3-0	Stevenson (og), Richardson, McMahon	11,183
11		23	(h)	Sunderland	W	3-1	Johnson, Sharp, Richardson	20,360
12		30	(a)	Southampton	L	2-3	Wright, King	18,141
13	Nov	6	(h)	Liverpool	L	0-5		52,741
14		13	(a)	Arsenal	D	1-1	King	23,067
15		20	(h)	West Brom A	D	0-0		16,001
16		27	(a)	West Ham U	L	0-2		21,424
17	Dec	4	(h)	Birmingham C	D	0-0		13,707
18		11	(a)	Ipswich T	W	2-0	Sheedy, Richardson	17,512
19		18	(h)	Luton T	W	5-0	Bailey, Sheedy, Curran, Heath 2	14,982
20		27	(a)	Stoke C	L	0-1		25,427
21		28	(h)	Nottingham F	W	3-1	Sharp 2 (1 pen), McMahon	25,147
22	Jan	1	(a)	West Brom A	D	2-2	Sharp, Higgins	15,194
23		3	(a)	Tottenham H	L	1-2	Sharp	28,455
24		15	(h)	Watford	W	1-0	Johnson	19,233
25		22	(a)	Norwich C	W	1-0	Ratcliffe	14,180
26	Feb	5	(h)	Notts Co	W	3-0	King, Heath, Sheedy	14,541
27		12	(a)	Aston Villa	L	0-2		21,117
28		26	(h)	Swansea C	D	2-2	King 2	17,112
29	Mar	2	(a)	Manchester C	D	0-0		22,253
30		5	(a)	Sunderland	L	1-2	Sharp	16,051
31		15	(h)	Southampton	W	2-0	Heath, Sheedy	15,002
32		19	(a)	Liverpool	D	0-0		44,737
33		26	(h)	Arsenal	L	2-3	Ainscow, Heath	16,318
34	Apr	2	(a)	Nottingham F	L	0-2		14,815
35		4	(h)	Stoke C	W	3-1	Sheedy 2, Sharp	15,360
36		9	(a)	Brighton & H.A.	W	2-1	Sheedy 2	14,534
37		19	(h)	Manchester U	W	2-0	Sharp, Heath	21,707
38		23	(a)	Birmingham C	L	0-1		11,045
39		30	(h)	West Ham U	W	2-0	Sharp 2	16,355
40	May	2	(h)	Coventry C	W	1-0	Sharp (pen)	12,972
41		7	(a)	Luton T	W	5-1	Johnson, Sheedy 2, Sharp 2 (1 pen)	12,447
42		14	(h)	Ipswich T	D	1-1	Wark (og)	17,420

FINAL LEAGUE POSITION: 7th in Division One

Appearances

Sub. Appearances

Goals

Southall	Borrows	Bailey	Higgins	Wright	Heath	McMahon	Johnson	Sharp	King	Sheedy	Richardson	Irvine	Ainscow	Walsh	Ratcliffe	Ross	Keeley	Arnold	Stevens	Curran	Reid	Mountfield	
1	2	3	4	5	6	7*	8	9	10	11	12												1
1	2	3	4	5	8	6		9	10	11	12	7*											2
1	2	3	4	5	8	6		9	10	11			7										3
1	2	3	4	5	8	6		9	10	11	12		7*										4
1	2	3	4	5	8	6		9	10	11			7										5
1	2			5	8	6		9	10	11		7*		3	4	12							6
1			4	5	8	6		9	10	11	2	12		3	7*								7
1	2	3	4	5	7	6	8	9	10	11													8
1	2	3	4	5	7	6	8	9	10	11													9
1	2	3	4	5		6	8	9	10	11	7												10
1	2	3	4	5	7*	6	8	9	10	11	12												11
1	2	3	4	5		6	8*	9	10	11	7	12											12
1	2	3		5	7	6	8*	9	10	11	12				4								13
			4	5	7	6	8	9	10	11*	12				3			1	2				14
			4	5	7	6	8	9	10	11					3			1	2				15
			4	5	8*	6	12	9	10	11		7			3			1	2				16
		3	4	5	8	6		9	10	11								1	2	7			17
		3	5		8	6	9			11	10				4			1	2	7			18
		3	5		8	6	9*	12		11	10				4			1	2	7			19
		3	5		8	6	9	12		11	10				4			1	2*	7			20
		3	5		12	6	9*	8		11					4			1	2	7	10		21
		3	5			6	9	8		11					4			1	2	7	10		22
		3	5			6	9	8		11					4			1	2	7	10		23
		3	5		7	6	12	8	9	11					4			1	2		10*		24
		3	5		8	6		9	7	11					4			1	2		10		25
		3	5		7*	12	8	9		11	6				4			1	2		10		26
		3	5		7	12	8	9		11	6				4			1	2		10*		27
		3	5		10	12	9	8		11	6	7*			4			1	2				28
		3	5		10	7	9	8		11	6				4			1	2				29
		3	5		10	7	9	8*		11	6	12			4			1	2				30
		3	5		10	8		9		11	6	7			4			1	2				31
		3	5		10	8		9		11	6	7*	12		4			1	2				32
		3	5		10	8		9		11	6	12	7		4			1	2*				33
		3	5		10	8	12	9		11	6*		7		4			1	2				34
		3	5		10	6	8	9		11	2		7		4			1					35
		3	5		10	8		9		11	6		7		4			1	2				36
		3	5		10	7	8	9		11	6				4			1	2				37
		3			10	7*	8	9		11	6		12		4			1	2			5	38
1		3	5		10		8	9		11	6		7		4				2				39
1		3	5		10	7	8*	9		11	6	12			4				2				40
1		3	5		10	7	8	9		11	6				4				2				41
1		3	5		10		8	9		11	6*	12	7		4				2				42
17	12	37	39	17	37	34	25	39	24	40	24	7	9	2	29	1	1	25	28	7	7	1	
					1		6	2			5	7	2				1						
		1	1	3	10	4	3	15	9	11	3	1	1		1				1				

31

1983-84

1	Aug	27	(h)	Stoke C	W	1-0	Sharp	22,658
2		29	(h)	West Ham U	L	0-1		20,375
3	Sep	3	(a)	Coventry C	D	1-1	Sheedy	12,532
4		6	(a)	Ipswich T	L	0-3		16,543
5		10	(h)	West Brom A	D	0-0		15,548
6		17	(a)	Tottenham H	W	2-1	Reid, Sheedy	29,125
7		24	(h)	Birmingham C	D	1-1	Sharp (pen)	15,253
8	Oct	1	(a)	Notts Co	W	1-0	Reid	7,949
9		15	(h)	Luton T	L	0-1		14,325
10		22	(h)	Watford	W	1-0	Johnson	13,571
11		29	(a)	Leicester C	L	0-2		10,953
12	Nov	6	(a)	Liverpool	L	0-3		40,875
13		12	(h)	Nottingham F	W	1-0	Heath	17,546
14		19	(a)	Arsenal	L	1-2	King (pen)	24,330
15		26	(h)	Norwich C	L	0-2		14,106
16	Dec	3	(a)	Manchester U	W	1-0	Sheedy	43,664
17		10	(h)	Aston Villa	D	1-1	Gray	15,810
18		17	(a)	Q.P.R.	L	0-2		11,608
19		26	(h)	Sunderland	D	0-0		18,683
20		27	(a)	Wolves	L	0-3		12,761
21		31	(h)	Coventry C	D	0-0		13,659
22	Jan	2	(a)	Birmingham C	W	2-0	Stevens, King	10,004
23		14	(a)	Stoke C	D	1-1	Heath	7,945
24		21	(h)	Tottenham H	W	2-1	Heath 2	18,003
25	Feb	4	(h)	Notts Co	W	4-1	Heath 3, Sheedy (pen)	13,016
26		11	(a)	West Brom A	D	1-1	Mountfield	10,313
27		25	(a)	Watford	D	4-4	Sharp 2, Gray, Heath	16,982
28	Mar	3	(h)	Liverpool	D	1-1	Harper	51,245
29		13	(a)	Nottingham F	L	0-1		13,647
30		17	(h)	Ipswich T	W	1-0	Mountfield	18,013
31		20	(h)	Leicester C	D	1-1	Richardson	15,142
32		31	(h)	Southampton	W	1-0	Gray	20,244
33	Apr	7	(a)	Luton T	W	3-0	Mountfield, Heath 2 (1 pen)	9,224
34		9	(h)	Arsenal	D	0-0		21,174
35		17	(a)	Southampton	L	1-3	Richardson	16,978
36		21	(a)	Sunderland	L	1-2	Heath	15,876
37		23	(h)	Wolves	W	2-0	Gray, Steven	17,185
38		28	(a)	Norwich C	D	1-1	Gray	13,624
39	May	5	(h)	Manchester U	D	1-1	Wakenshaw	28,817
40		7	(a)	Aston Villa	W	2-0	Richardson, Sharp	16,792
41		12	(h)	Q.P.R.	W	3-1	Heath, Sharp 2	20,679
42		14	(a)	West Ham U	W	1-0	Richardson	25,452

FINAL LEAGUE POSITION: 7th in Division One

Appearances

Sub. Appearances

Goals

Arnold	Harper	Bailey	Mountfield	Higgins	Richardson	Steven	Heath	Sharp	King	Sheedy	Johnson	Ratcliffe	Curran	Reid	Southall	Irvine	Gray	Stevens	Hughes	Rimmer	Wakenshaw	Bishop	
1	2	3	4	5	6	7	8	9	10	11													1
1	2	3	4	5	6*	7	8	9	10	11	12												2
1	2	3		5	6	7	8*	9	10	11	12	4											3
1	2	3*		5	6	8		9		11	10	4	7	12									4
1	2	3		5	12	6	8	9		11	10	4	7*										5
1	2	3		5	12	7	8	9		11	10	4		6*									6
1	2	3		5		7*	8	9	12	11	10	4		6									7
	2	3		5		7	8	9		11		4		6	1	10							8
	2	3		5		7	8	9	10	11		4		6	1								9
	2	3		5	6	7*		9	10	11	8	4			1	12							10
	2	3		5	6	7	8	9	10	11*		4			1	12							11
	2	3		5		6	8	9	10	11		4			1	7							12
	2	3		5			8		10	11		4		6	1	7	9						13
	2	3	5				8		10	11		4		6	1	7	9						14
	2	3	5				8*		10	11		4		6	1	7	9	12					15
			4	5			8	9		11		3		6	1	7	10	2					16
	12	3	5				8		10*	11		4		6	1	7	9	2					17
		3	5				8		10	11	9	4		6	1	7		2					18
		3	5				8			11	10	4		6	1	7	9	2					19
			5				8	12		11*		4		6	1	7	9	2	3	10			20
		3	5		12		8*		10	11		4		6	1	7	9	2					21
		3	5				8		10	11		4		6	1	7	9	2					22
		3	5		2		8	9		11		4		6	1	7	10						23
		3	5		10		8	9		11		4		6	1	7		2					24
		3	5		10		8			11		4		6	1	7	9	2					25
		3	5		10		8			11		4		6	1	7	9	2					26
		3	5				8	9		11		4		6	1	7	10	2					27
	12	3	5			7*	8	9		11		4		6	1		10	2					28
	11	3	5				8	9				4		6	1	7	10	2					29
		3	5		11	12	8	9*				4		6	1	7	10	2					30
		3	5		11	7	8		10			4		6	1		9	2					31
	7*	3	5		11	12	8	9				4		6	1		10	2					32
	4	3	5		11	10	8	9					7	6	1			2					33
		3	5		11	12	8	9*				4	7	6	1		10	2					34
		3	5		11	10	8					4	7	6	1		9	2					35
	12	3	5		11	10	8	9				4	7	6*	1			2					36
		3	5		11	10	8					4	7	6	1		9	2					37
		3	5		11	10	8	12				4	7*	6	1		9	2					38
	4	3	5		11	10		9	8					6	1			2			7*	12	39
		3	5		11	10	8	9	7			4		6	1			2					40
		3	5		11	7	8	9				4		6	1		10	2					41
		3	5		11	7	8	9	10			4		6	1			2					42
7	26	33	31	14	25	23	36	27	19	28	7	38	8	34	35	19	23	26	1	1	1		
	3			3	4			1	1		2			1			2	1			1		
	1		3	4	1	12	7	2	4	1				2		5	1				1		

1984-85

1	Aug	25	(h)	Tottenham H	L	1-4	Heath (pen)	35,630
2		27	(a)	West Brom A	L	1-2	Heath (pen)	13,464
3	Sep	31	(a)	Chelsea	W	1-0	Richardson	17,734
4		4	(h)	Ipswich T	D	1-1	Heath	22,314
5		8	(h)	Coventry C	W	2-1	Sharp, Steven	20,013
6		15	(a)	Newcastle U	W	3-2	Gray, Sheedy, Steven	26,944
7		22	(h)	Southampton	D	2-2	Mountfield, Sharp	22,354
8		29	(a)	Watford	W	5-4	Heath 2, Mountfield, Sharp, Steven	18,335
9	Oct	6	(a)	Arsenal	L	0-1		37,049
10		13	(h)	Aston Villa	W	2-1	Heath, Sharp	25,089
11		20	(a)	Liverpool	W	1-0	Sharp	45,545
12		27	(h)	Manchester U	W	5-0	Heath, Sharp, Sheedy 2, Stevens	40,769
13	Nov	3	(h)	Leicester C	W	3-0	Heath, Sheedy, Steven	27,784
14		10	(a)	West Ham U	W	1-0	Heath	24,089
15		17	(h)	Stoke C	W	4-0	Heath 2, Reid, Steven	26,705
16		24	(a)	Norwich C	L	2-4	Sharp, Sheedy	16,925
17	Dec	1	(h)	Sheffield W	D	1-1	Sharp (pen)	35,440
18		8	(a)	Q.P.R.	D	0-0		14,338
19		15	(h)	Nottingham F	W	5-0	Reid, Sharp 2, Sheedy, Steven	22,487
20		22	(h)	Chelsea	L	3-4	Bracewell, Sharp 2 (1 pen)	29,887
21		26	(a)	Sunderland	W	2-1	Mountfield 2	19,714
22		29	(a)	Ipswich T	W	2-0	Sharp 2	16,045
23	Jan	1	(h)	Luton T	W	2-1	Steven 2	31,682
24		12	(h)	Newcastle U	W	4-0	Mountfield, Sharp, Sheedy 2	32,156
25	Feb	2	(h)	Watford	W	4-0	Sheedy, Stevens 2, Steven	34,026
26		23	(a)	Leicester C	W	2-1	Gray 2	17,345
27	Mar	2	(a)	Manchester U	D	1-1	Mountfield	51,150
28		16	(a)	Aston Villa	D	1-1	Richardson	22,625
29		23	(h)	Arsenal	W	2-0	Gray, Sharp	36,389
30		30	(a)	Southampton	W	2-1	Richardson 2	18,754
31	Apr	3	(a)	Tottenham H	W	2-1	Gray, Steven	48,108
32		6	(h)	Sunderland	W	4-1	Gray 2, Sharp, Steven	35,978
33		16	(h)	West Brom A	W	4-1	Atkins, Sharp 2 (1 pen), Sheedy	29,750
34		20	(a)	Stoke C	W	2-0	Sharp, Sheedy	18,285
35		27	(h)	Norwich C	W	3-0	Bracewell, Mountfield, Steven	32,085
36	May	4	(a)	Sheffield W	W	1-0	Gray	37,381
37		6	(h)	Q.P.R.	W	2-0	Mountfield, Sharp	50,514
38		8	(h)	West Ham U	W	3-0	Gray, Mountfield 2	32,657
39		11	(a)	Nottingham F	L	0-1		18,784
40		23	(h)	Liverpool	W	1-0	Wilkinson	15,045
41		26	(a)	Coventry C	L	1-4	Wilkinson	21,224
42		28	(a)	Luton T	L	0-2		11,509

FINAL LEAGUE POSITION: 1st in Division One

Appearances

Sub. Appearances

Goals

Southall	Stevens	Bailey	Ratcliffe	Mountfield	Reid	Steven	Heath	Sharp	Bracewell	Richardson	Gray	Curran	Sheedy	Van Den Hauwe	Harper	Atkins	Wilkinson	Oldroyd	Wakenshaw	Hughes	Morrissey	Danskin	Walsh	Rimmer	
1	2	3	4	5	6	7	8	9	10	11*	12														1
1	2	3	4	5	6	10	8	9		11		7													2
1	2	3	4	5	6	7	8	9	10	11															3
1	2	3	4	5	6	7	8	9	10	11*	12														4
1	2	3	4	5	6	7	8	9	10	11*	12														5
1	2	3	4	5	6	7	8		10		9		11												6
1	2	3	4	5	6	7	8	9	10				11												7
1	2	3	4	5	6	7	8	9	10			12	11*												8
1	2		4	5	6	7	8	9	10	11				3											9
1	2		4	5	6	7	8	9	10					3	11										10
1	2		4	5	6	7	8	9	10					3	11										11
1	2		4	5	6	7	8	9	10		12		11*	3											12
1	2		4	5	6	7	8	9*	10		12		11	3											13
1	2		4	5	6	7	8	9	10				11	3											14
1	2		4	5	6	7	8	9	10				11	3											15
1	2		4	5	6	7	8	9	10		12		11	3*											16
1	2		4	5	6	7	8*	9	10		12		11	3											17
1	2		4	5	6	7		9	10		8		11	3											18
1	2		4	5	6	7		9	10		8*	12	11	3											19
1	2	3	4	5	6	7		9	10		8		11												20
1		3	4	5	6	7		9	10		8		11			2									21
1		3	4	5	6	7		9	10		8		11		2										22
1	2		4	5	6	7		9	10		8		11	3											23
1	2		4	5	6	7		9	10		8		11	3											24
1	2		4	5	6	7*		9	10		8	12	11	3											25
1	2		4	5	6	7			10		9		11	3	8										26
1	2		4	5	6	7			10		9	8	11	3											27
1	2		4	5		7	8		10	6	9			3	11										28
1	2		4	5	6	7	8			11	9			3	10										29
1	2		4	5	6	7	8*		10	11	9			3			12								30
1	2		4	5	6	7	8		10		9*		11	3	12										31
1	2	3	4	5	6	7	8		10		9		11*		12										32
1	2		4		6	7	8		10		9		11	3	12	5*									33
1	2		4		6	7	8		10		9		11	3		5									34
1	2		4	5		7	8		10	6	9			3	11										35
1	2		4	5	6	7	8		10		9		11	3											36
1	2		4	5	6	7	8		10		9		11	3											37
1	2			5	6	7	8		10	12	9*		11	3		4									38
1	2		4	5		7					6		11	3	8*	10	9	12							39
1	2	3	4								6	9	11	5	7	10*	8		12						40
1			4			7		9	10		6		11	3	2		8			5					41
1		3									6		5	4			9*		8	2	7	10	11	12	42
42	37	15	40	37	36	40	17	36	37	14	21	4	29	31	10	6	4	1	2	1	1	1			
											1	5	5			3	1	1				1			
	3			10	2	12	11	21	2	4	9		11			1	2								

1985-86

1	Aug	17	(a)	Leicester C	L	1-3	Mountfield	16,932
2		20	(h)	West Brom A	W	2-0	Heath 2	26,788
3		24	(h)	Coventry C	D	1-1	Sharp	27,691
4		26	(a)	Tottenham H	W	1-0	Lineker	29,720
5		31	(h)	Birmingham C	W	4-1	Lineker 3, Steven (pen)	28,066
6	Sep	3	(a)	Sheffield W	W	5-1	Mountfield, Lineker 2, Steven, Heath	30,065
7		7	(a)	Q.P.R.	L	0-3		16,544
8		14	(h)	Luton T	W	2-0	Sheedy, Sharp	26,419
9		21	(h)	Liverpool	L	2-3	Sharp, Lineker	51,509
10		28	(a)	Aston Villa	D	0-0		22,048
11	Oct	5	(h)	Oxford U	W	2-0	Sharp, Bracewell	24,553
12		12	(a)	Chelsea	L	1-2	Sheedy	27,634
13		19	(h)	Watford	W	4-1	Heath, Sharp 2, Bracewell	26,425
14		26	(a)	Manchester C	D	1-1	Heath	28,807
15	Nov	2	(a)	West Ham U	L	1-2	Steven	23,844
16		9	(h)	Arsenal	W	6-1	Lineker 2, Heath 2, Steven (pen), Sharp	28,620
17		16	(a)	Ipswich T	W	4-3	Heath, Sharp, Sheedy, Steven (pen)	13,910
18		23	(h)	Nottingham F	D	1-1	Bracewell	27,860
19		30	(a)	Southampton	W	3-2	Lineker, Heath, Steven	16,917
20	Dec	7	(a)	West Brom A	W	3-0	Sheedy, Van Den Hauwe, Lineker	12,206
21		14	(h)	Leicester C	L	1-2	Richardson	23,347
22		21	(a)	Coventry C	W	3-1	Lineker 2, Sharp	11,059
23		26	(h)	Manchester U	W	3-1	Sharp 2, Lineker	42,551
24		28	(h)	Sheffield W	W	3-1	Stevens, Lineker 2	41,536
25	Jan	1	(a)	Newcastle U	D	2-2	Steven, Sharp (pen)	27,820
26		11	(h)	Q.P.R.	W	4-3	Sharp 2 (1 pen), Lineker, Wilkinson	26,015
27		18	(a)	Birmingham C	W	2-0	Lineker 2	10,502
28	Feb	1	(h)	Tottenham H	W	1-0	Reid	33,178
29		11	(h)	Manchester C	W	4-0	Lineker 3, Sharp	30,006
30		22	(a)	Liverpool	W	2-0	Ratcliffe, Lineker	45,445
31	Mar	1	(h)	Aston Villa	W	2-0	Sharp, Lineker	32,133
32		16	(h)	Chelsea	D	1-1	Sheedy	30,145
33		22	(a)	Luton T	L	1-2	Richardson	10,949
34		29	(h)	Newcastle U	W	1-0	Richardson	41,116
35		31	(a)	Manchester U	D	0-0		51,189
36	Apr	12	(a)	Arsenal	W	1-0	Heath	28,251
37		15	(a)	Watford	W	2-0	Lineker, Sharp	18,960
38		19	(h)	Ipswich T	W	1-0	Sharp	39,055
39		26	(a)	Nottingham F	D	0-0		30,171
40		30	(a)	Oxford U	L	0-1		13,939
41	May	3	(h)	Southampton	W	6-1	Mountfield, Steven, Lineker 3, Sharp	33,057
42		5	(h)	West Ham U	W	3-1	Lineker 2, Steven (pen)	40,073

FINAL LEAGUE POSITION: 2nd in Division One

Appearances

Sub. Appearances

Goals

Southall	Stevens	Van Den Hauwe	Ratcliffe	Mountfield	Reid	Steven	Lineker	Sharp	Bracewell	Sheedy	Heath	Marshall	Harper	Atkins	Richardson	Bailey	Mimms	Pointon	Wilkinson	Billinge	Aspinall	#
1	2	3	4	5	6	7	8	9	10	11*	12											1
1	2	3	4			7	8		10	11	9	5	6									2
1	2	3				7	8	9	10	11*	6	5	4	12								3
1	2	3	4			7	8	12	10	11	9*	5	6									4
1	2	3	4	5	6	7	8		10	11	9											5
1	2	3	4	5	6*	7	8	9	10	11	12											6
1	2	3	4	5	6	7	8	9	10		11											7
1	2	3	4	5		7	8	12	10	11	9*		6									8
1	2	3	4	5		7	8	9	10	11	12	5*	6									9
1	2	3	4			7	8	9	10	11		5	6									10
1	2	3	4			7	8	9	10	11		5	6									11
1	2	5	4			7	8	9	10	11	12				6*	3						12
1	2	3	4			7	8	9	10	11	6	5*	12									13
	2	5	4			7	8	9	10	11*	6		3		12		1					14
1	2	5	4			7	8	9	10	11	6		3									15
1	5		4			7	8	9	10	11	6		2						3			16
1	5	3	4			7	8	9	10	11	6		2									17
1	5	3	4			7	8	9	10	11	6		2									18
1	5	3	4			7	8		10	11	6		2						9			19
1	5	3	4			7	8		10*	11	6		2					12	9			20
1	2		4			7	8	9	10		6	5			11			3				21
1	2	5	4			7	8	9	10	11	6							3				22
1	2	5	4			7	8	9	10	11	6							3				23
1	2	5	4			7	8	9	10	11	6*		12					3				24
1	2	5	4			7	8	9	10*	11	6		12					3				25
1	2	5	4				8	9		11*	6		7		10			3	12			26
1	2	5	4			7	8	9		11	6				10			3				27
1	2	5	4		6	7	8	9	10						11			3				28
1	2	5	4		6	7	8	9	10	11*					12			3				29
1	2	5	4		6	7	8	9	10*				12		11			3				30
1	2	5	4		6	7	8	9			10				11			3				31
1	2	4		5		7	8	9	10	11	12				6*			3				32
1		4		5		7	8	9	10	11*	12		2		6			3				33
	2	3*	4	5	6	7	8	9	10		12				11		1					34
	2	3	4	5	6	7	8*	9	10		12				11		1					35
	2	3	4	5	6	7	8*	9	10		12				11		1					36
	2	3	4	5	6	7	8*	9	10		12				11		1					37
	2	3	4	5	6	7		9	10		8				11		1					38
	2	3	4	5	6	7	8	9	10	11*	12						1					39
	2	3	4	5		7	8	9	10	11	12				6*		1					40
	2	3	4	5	6	7	8	9	10*	11	12						1					41
	2	3	4			7	8*			11	10				6		1		9	5	12	42
32	41	40	39	15	15	41	41	35	38	31	24	8	17		16	1	10	14	3	1		
								2			12	1	4	1	2			1	1		1	
	1	1	1	3	1	9	30	19	3	5	10				3			1				

37

1986-87

1	Aug	23	(h)	Nottingham F	W	2-0	Sheedy 2		35,198
2		25	(a)	Sheffield W	D	2-2	Sharp, Langley		33,007
3		30	(a)	Coventry C	D	1-1	Marshall		13,504
4	Sep	2	(h)	Oxford U	W	3-1	Steven (pen), Harper, Langley		26,018
5		6	(h)	Q.P.R.	D	0-0			30,173
6		13	(a)	Wimbledon	W	2-1	Sheedy, Sharp		11,708
7		21	(h)	Manchester U	W	3-1	Sharp, Sheedy, Heath		25,843
8		27	(a)	Tottenham H	L	0-2			28,007
9	Oct	4	(h)	Arsenal	L	0-1			30,007
10		11	(a)	Charlton Ath	L	2-3	Sheedy 2		10,564
11		18	(a)	Southampton	W	2-0	Steven (pen), Wilkinson		18,009
12		25	(h)	Watford	W	3-2	Mountfield 2, Steven (pen)		28,577
13	Nov	2	(a)	West Ham U	L	0-1			19,094
14		8	(h)	Chelsea	D	2-2	Steven (pen), Sheedy		29,727
15		15	(a)	Leicester C	W	2-0	Heath, Sheedy		13,450
16		23	(h)	Liverpool	D	0-0			48,247
17		29	(a)	Manchester C	W	3-1	Heath 2, Power		27,097
18	Dec	6	(h)	Norwich C	W	4-0	Power, Steven (pen), Pointon, Heath		26,746
19		13	(a)	Luton T	L	0-1			11,151
20		20	(h)	Wimbledon	W	3-0	Steven, Sheedy, Heath		25,553
21		26	(a)	Newcastle U	W	4-0	Power, Steven 2, Heath		35,079
22		28	(h)	Leicester C	W	5-1	Heath 2, Wilkinson, O'Neill (og), Sheedy		39,730
23	Jan	1	(h)	Aston Villa	W	3-0	Harper, Steven, Sheedy		40,203
24		3	(a)	Q.P.R.	W	1-0	Sharp		19,297
25		17	(h)	Sheffield W	W	2-0	Steven (pen), Watson		33,011
26		25	(a)	Nottingham F	L	0-1			17,009
27	Feb	7	(h)	Coventry C	W	3-1	Stevens, Steven (pen), Heath		30,402
28		14	(a)	Oxford U	D	1-1	Wilkinson		11,878
29		28	(a)	Manchester U	D	0-0			47,421
30	Mar	8	(a)	Watford	L	1-2	Heath		14,014
31		14	(h)	Southampton	W	3-0	Wright (og), Power, Watson		26,564
32		21	(h)	Charlton Ath	W	2-1	Steven (pen), Stevens		27,291
33		28	(a)	Arsenal	W	1-0	Clarke		36,218
34	Apr	4	(a)	Chelsea	W	2-1	McLaughlin (og), Harper		21,914
35		11	(h)	West Ham U	W	4-0	Clarke, Reid, Stevens, Watson		35,731
36		18	(a)	Aston Villa	W	1-0	Sheedy		31,218
37		20	(h)	Newcastle U	W	3-0	Clarke 3		43,576
38		25	(a)	Liverpool	L	1-3	Sheedy		44,827
39	May	2	(h)	Manchester C	D	0-0			37,541
40		4	(a)	Norwich C	W	1-0	Van Den Hauwe		23,489
41		9	(h)	Luton T	W	3-1	Steven 2 (2 pens), Sharp		44,092
42		11	(h)	Tottenham H	W	1-0	Mountfield		28,287

FINAL LEAGUE POSITION: 1st in Division One

Appearances

Sub. Appearances

Goals

Mimms	Harper	Power	Ratcliffe	Watson	Langley	Steven	Heath	Sharp	Richardson	Sheedy	Wilkinson	Marshall	Adams	Mountfield	Aspinall	Southall	Pointon	Stevens	Reid	Snodin	Van Den Hauwe	Clarke	
1	2	3	4	5	6	7	8	9	10*	11	12												1
1	2	3	4	5	6	7	8	9		11	10												2
1	2	3	4	5	6*	7	8	9		11		12	10										3
1	2	3	4	5	6	7	8	9		11			10										4
1	2	3	4	5	6	7	8	9		11		12	10*										5
1	2	3	4	5	6	7	8*	9		11	12			10									6
1		3	4	5	6	7	8	9		11*	10	12	2										7
1		3	4	5	6	7	8	9		11*	10	12	2										8
1		3	4	5	6	7		9		11	10		8	2*	12								9
1	2	3	4	5	6*	8	10	9		11	12		7										10
1	2	3	4	5*	11	7	8	9		10			6	12									11
	2	3	4	6		10	8	9		11			7	5		1							12
	2	3	4	6*		7	8	9		11	10			5	12	1							13
	2	3	4	6		7	8	9		11	10			5		1							14
	2	3	4	6		7*	8	9		11	10			5	12	1							15
	2	3	4	6*		7	8	9		11	12		10	5		1							16
	2	6*	4			7	8	9		11	12		10	5		1	3						17
	10	6	4	5		7	8	9*		11	12					1	3	2					18
	10	6	4	5		7	8	9		11	12					1	3*	2					19
	10	6	4	5		7	8	9		11						1	3*	2	12				20
	10	6	4	5		7	8	9*		11	12					1	3	2					21
	10	6*	4	5		7	8			11	9				12	1	3	2					22
	10	6*	4	5		7	8			11	9				12	1	3	2					23
	10	6	4	5		7	8	9		11						1	3	2					24
	10	6	4	5*		7	8	9		11						1	3	2	12				25
	10	3*	4			7	8			11	9			5		1	12	2	6				26
	12	11	4	5		7	8	9*								1		2	6	10	3		27
	12	11	4	5		7	8			9						1		2	6	10	3*		28
	8	11	4	5		7	8			12						1		2	6*	10	3		29
		11	4	5		7	8			12						1		2	6	10	3*	9	30
	12	11	4	5		7	8									1		2	6*	10	3	9	31
	12	11	4	5		7	8									1		2	6	10	3*	9	32
	12	11	4	5		7	8									1		2	6	10	3	9*	33
	10	3	4	5		7	8			11*						1	12	2	6		9		34
	10	3	4	5		7	8			11						1		2	6		9		35
	12	3	4	5		7	8			11*						1		2	6	10	9		36
	6	11	4	5		7	8									1	3	2		10	9		37
		3	4	5		7	8			11						1		2	6	10	9		38
	12	11	4	5		7	8									1		2	6*	10	3	9	39
		11	4	5		7	8	9								1		2	6	10	3		40
	11		4	5		7	8	9								1		2	6	10	3		41
	7		4	5			8*	9					11	12		1		2	6	10	3		42
11	29	40	42	35	16	41	41	27	1	28	12		10	12		31	10	25	15	15	10	10	
	7										10	2	2	1	6		2		1	1			
	3	4		3	2	14	11	5		13	3	1		3			1	3	1		1	5	

1987-88

1	Aug	15	(h)	Norwich C	W	1-0	Power	31,728
2		18	(a)	Wimbledon	D	1-1	Sharp	7,763
3		22	(a)	Nottingham F	D	0-0		20,445
4		29	(h)	Sheffield W	W	4-0	Clarke 2, Steven 2 (1 pen)	29,649
5	Sep	2	(a)	Q.P.R.	L	0-1		15,380
6		5	(h)	Tottenham H	D	0-0		32,389
7		12	(a)	Luton T	L	1-2	Pointon	8,124
8		19	(h)	Manchester U	W	2-1	Clarke 2	38,439
9		26	(h)	Coventry C	L	1-2	Clarke	28,153
10	Oct	3	(a)	Southampton	W	4-0	Sharp 4	15,719
11		10	(h)	Chelsea	W	4-1	Sharp 2, Heath 2	32,004
12		17	(a)	Newcastle U	D	1-1	Snodin	20,266
13		24	(h)	Watford	W	2-0	Heath, Sharp	28,501
14	Nov	1	(a)	Liverpool	L	0-2		44,760
15		14	(h)	West Ham U	W	3-1	Watson, Reid, Sharp	29,405
16		21	(a)	Portsmouth	W	1-0	Sharp	17,724
17		28	(h)	Oxford U	D	0-0		25,443
18	Dec	5	(a)	Charlton Ath	D	0-0		7,208
19		12	(h)	Derby Co	W	3-0	Snodin, Steven (pen), Heath	26,224
20		19	(a)	Arsenal	D	1-1	Watson	34,857
21		26	(h)	Luton T	W	2-0	Heath 2	32,242
22		28	(a)	Manchester U	L	1-2	Watson	47,024
23	Jan	1	(a)	Sheffield W	L	0-1		26,443
24		3	(h)	Nottingham F	W	1-0	Clarke	21,680
25		16	(a)	Norwich C	W	3-0	Sharp 2, Heath	15,750
26	Feb	13	(h)	Q.P.R.	W	2-0	Parker (og), Pointon	24,724
27		27	(h)	Southampton	W	1-0	Power	20,764
28	Mar	5	(h)	Newcastle U	W	1-0	Clarke	25,674
29		9	(a)	Tottenham H	L	1-2	Fenwick (og)	18,662
30		12	(a)	Chelsea	D	0-0		17,390
31		20	(h)	Liverpool	W	1-0	Clarke	44,162
32		26	(a)	Watford	W	2-1	Sheedy, Clarke	13,503
33		29	(h)	Wimbledon	D	2-2	Steven (pen), Pointon	20,351
34	Apr	4	(a)	West Ham U	D	0-0		21,195
35		9	(h)	Portsmouth	W	2-1	Heath, Steven	21,292
36		19	(h)	Coventry C	W	2-1	Sharp, Heath	15,641
37		23	(a)	Oxford U	D	1-1	Clarke	7,619
38		30	(h)	Charlton Ath	D	1-1	Steven (pen)	20,372
39	May	2	(a)	Derby Co	D	0-0		17,974
40		7	(h)	Arsenal	L	1-2	Watson	22,445

FINAL LEAGUE POSITION: 4th in Division One

Appearances

Sub. Appearances

Goals

#	Mimms	Van Den Hauwe	Pointon	Ratcliffe	Watson	Harper	Steven	Clarke	Sharp	Adams	Power	Marshall	Mountfield	Reid	Snodin	Sheedy	Heath	Southall	Wilson	Stevens	Jones
1	1	2	3	4	5	6	7	8	9	10	11										
2	1	2	3	4	5	6		8	9	7	11	10*	12								
3	1	2	3	4	5		7	8	9*		11	12		6	10						
4	1		3	4	5	2	7	8	9		11*			6	10	12					
5	1		3	4	5	2	7	8*	9		11†		12	6	10	14					
6	1	3	11	4	5	2	7	8*	9					6	10		12				
7		3	11*	4	5	2	7		9†		14	12		6	10		8	1			
8		3	11	4	5	2	7		9					6	10		8	1			
9		2*	3	4	5	6†	7	8	9				14		10		12	1	11		
10		3		4	5	12	7	8†	9					6	10		14	1	11*	2	
11	1	3		4	5		7		9					6	10		8		11	2	
12	1	3		4	5	12	7		9					6	10		8		11	2*	
13			3	4	5		7		9					6	10		8	1	11	2	
14		3		4	5		7	8*	9				12	6	10			1	11	2	
15		3		4	5	12	7*		9					6	10	11†	8	1	14	2	
16		3	12	4	5		7	14	9					6	10	11†	8*	1		2	
17		3		4	5		7		9					6	10*	11	8	1	12	2	
18			3	4	5		7		9	12				6	10	11	8*	1		2	
19			3	4	5		7		9					6	10	11	8	1		2	
20			3	4	5		7		9					6	10	11*	8	1	12	2	
21			3	4	5		7		9					6	10		8	1	11	2	
22			3	4	5		7	12	9					6	10		8	1	11*	2	
23			3	4	5		7	12	9					6	10		8*	1	11	2	
24		3		4	5		7		9					6	10		8	1	11	2	
25		4	3		5	12	7		9					6*	10		8	1	11	2	
26		4	3		5	12	7†		9		11		14	6	10*		8	1		2	
27			3		5	4		8	9	7*	11				10		6	1		2	12
28		4	3		5	6	7	8	9	10						11		1		2	
29		4	3		5	6	7	8	9	10†	14					11	12	1	2*		
30		4	3		5	6	7	8	9		10					11		1		2	
31		4	3		5	10	7	8*	9		14			6		11†	12	1		2	
32		4	3			6	7	8	9		10		5			11		1		2	
33			3			4	7	8			10		5	6		11	9	1		2	
34		4	3			10	7	8*					5	6	12	11	9	1		2	
35		4	3		5	10	7							6	8	11	9	1		2	
36		4	3		5		7	8	9					6	10*		12	1	11	2	
37		4	3		5	14	7	8	9					6	12		10†	1	11*	2	
38		4	3		5	10	7		9		11			6			8	1		2	
39			3		5	8	7	9			11		4	6	10			1		2	
40		4	3		5	12	7	8*	9		11			6	10†	14		1		2	
	8	28	32	24	37	21	36	24	32	7	12	1	4	32	29	14	23	32	13	31	
			1		7		3			1	2	1	5		2	3	6		3		1
			3		4	6	10	13		2				1	2	1	9				

41

1988-89

1	Aug	27	(h)	Newcastle U	W	4-0	Cottee 3, Sharp	41,560
2	Sep	3	(a)	Coventry C	W	1-0	Cottee	18,625
3		10	(h)	Nottingham F	D	1-1	Heath	34,003
4		17	(a)	Millwall	L	1-2	McLeary (og)	17,507
5		24	(h)	Luton T	L	0-2		26,017
6	Oct	1	(a)	Wimbledon	L	1-2	Heath	6,367
7		8	(h)	Southampton	W	4-1	Cottee 2, Watson, Steven	25,356
8		22	(a)	Aston Villa	L	0-2		26,636
9		30	(h)	Manchester U	D	1-1	Cottee	27,005
10	Nov	5	(a)	Sheffield W	D	1-1	Steven (pen)	21,761
11		12	(a)	Charlton Ath	W	2-1	Sharp, Reid	8,627
12		19	(h)	Norwich C	D	1-1	Steven (pen)	28,118
13		26	(a)	West Ham U	W	1-0	Steven	22,176
14	Dec	3	(h)	Tottenham H	W	1-0	Cottee	29,657
15		11	(a)	Liverpool	D	1-1	Clarke (pen)	42,372
16		17	(a)	Q.P.R.	D	0-0		10,067
17		26	(h)	Middlesbrough	W	2-1	Steven, Cottee	32,651
18		31	(h)	Coventry C	W	3-1	Sheedy 2, Bracewell	30,790
19	Jan	2	(a)	Nottingham F	L	0-2		26,008
20		14	(h)	Arsenal	L	1-3	Watson	34,825
21		21	(a)	Luton T	L	0-1		9,013
22	Feb	4	(h)	Wimbledon	D	1-1	Sharp (pen)	23,365
23		11	(a)	Southampton	D	1-1	Sheedy	15,845
24		14	(h)	Aston Villa	D	1-1	Cottee	20,142
25		25	(a)	Derby Co	L	2-3	Sharp, Clarke	17,103
26	Mar	11	(h)	Sheffield W	W	1-0	Cottee	22,542
27		22	(a)	Newcastle U	L	0-2		20,933
28		25	(h)	Millwall	D	1-1	Sheedy	27,062
29		27	(a)	Middlesbrough	D	3-3	Cottee, Sheedy, Nevin	31,351
30	Apr	1	(h)	Q.P.R.	W	4-1	Clarke, Sheedy (pen), Cottee, Steven	23,028
31		8	(a)	Arsenal	L	0-2		37,608
32		10	(h)	Charlton Ath	W	3-2	Sharp, Sheedy, Nevin	16,316
33		22	(a)	Tottenham H	L	1-2	McDonald	28,568
34	May	3	(h)	Liverpool	D	0-0		45,994
35		6	(a)	Norwich C	L	0-1		13,239
36		10	(a)	Manchester U	W	2-1	Sharp 2	26,722
37		13	(h)	West Ham U	W	3-1	Sheedy, Watson, Bracewell	21,694
38		15	(h)	Derby Co	W	1-0	Wilson	17,826

FINAL LEAGUE POSITION: 8th in Division One

Appearances

Sub. Appearances

Goals

Southall	McDonald	Pointon	Snodin	Watson	Reid	Steven	McCall	Sharp	Cottee	Nevin	Sheedy	Heath	Wilson	Clarke	Van Den Hauwe	Ratcliffe	Bracewell	Ebbrell	
1	2	3	4	5	6	7*	8	9	10	11	12								1
1	2	3	4	5	6		8	9	10	7	11								2
1	2	3	4	5	6		8	9	10	7*	11†	12	14						3
1	2	3	4	5	6		8*	9	10		11†	7		12	14				4
1	2*		4	5	6		8	9	10		11	7	3	12					5
1	2	3	4		6		8	9	10		11	7			5				6
1			2	5	6	11	8	9	10			7			3	4			7
1	12		2	5	6	11†	8	9	10			7	14		3*	4			8
1			2	5	6	11	8	9	10		7*	12			3	4			9
1			2	5	6	7	8	9	10			11			3	4			10
1			2	5	6	7	8	9	10			11			3	4			11
1			2	5	6	7	8	9	10			11			3	4			12
1			2	5	6	7	8	9	10			11			3	4			13
1			2	5		7	8	9*	10			11	12		3	4	6		14
1			2	5	12	7	8		10			11	9		3	4	6*		15
1			2	5		7	8		10	11*	12		9		3	4	6		16
1	3	2	5	14		7	8		10*	9	11†		12			4	6		17
1	12	2	5	8	7				10	9	11				3*	4	6		18
1	3	2	5	8	7				10	9*	11	12				4	6		19
1	14	3	2	5	8*		12		10	7	11†		9			4	6		20
1	14	3	2	5		8†			10	7*	11	12	9			4	6		21
1	2		5		6	8	9		10	7		11*			3	4	12		22
1	2		5		7	8	9		10†	14	11	6*	12		3	4			23
1	2		5		7	8	9		10	12	11				3*	4	6		24
1	2	3	6	5	7	8	9*			12	11		10						25
1	14	3	2†	5		7	8		10	12	11*		9			4	6		26
1	2	3				7	8*	9	10†	14	11		12	5		4	6		27
1	2	3				7	14	9	12	8	11†		10*	5		4	6		28
1	2	3				7			10*	8	11	12	9	5		4	6		29
1	2	3	5			7			10	8	11		9			4	6		30
1	2	3		7*	5				10	8	11		9		4	6	12		31
1	2	3					8	9		7*	11		10	5	4	6	12		32
1	2		5	8	14			9	10	7	11†		12		3	4	6*		33
1	2		5	8	12			9	10	7	11*				3	4	6		34
1	2	3	5	8	7				10		11		9			4	6		35
1	2	12	5	8	6			9	10	7	11				3*	4			36
1	2	3	5	8				9	10	7	11*		12			4	6		37
1	2	3	5		6			9*	10	7	11		12				8		38
38	22	20	23	32	16	29	29	26	35	20	24	6	11	12	24	30	20	1	
	3	3		2		4			1	5	2	1	7	8	1		3		
		1		3	1	6		7	13	2	8	2	1	3		2			

43

1989-90

1	Aug	19	(a)	Coventry C	L	0-2		17,981
2		22	(h)	Tottenham H	W	2-1	Newell, Sheedy	34,402
3		26	(h)	Southampton	W	3-0	Whiteside, Newell, McCall	27,807
4		30	(a)	Sheffield W	D	1-1	Sheedy	19,657
5	Sep	9	(h)	Manchester U	W	3-2	Newell, Nevin, Sharp	37,916
6		16	(a)	Charlton Ath	W	1-0	Newell	11,491
7		23	(h)	Liverpool	L	1-3	Newell	42,453
8		30	(a)	Crystal Palace	L	1-2	Newell	15,943
9	Oct	14	(h)	Millwall	W	2-1	Sheedy (pen), Whiteside	26,125
10		21	(h)	Arsenal	W	3-0	Nevin 2, McDonald	32,917
11		28	(a)	Norwich C	D	1-1	Cottee	18,627
12	Nov	5	(a)	Aston Villa	L	2-6	Cottee, McGrath (og)	17,637
13		11	(h)	Chelsea	L	0-1		33,737
14		18	(h)	Wimbledon	D	1-1	Sheedy (pen)	21,561
15		25	(a)	Nottingham F	L	0-1		20,709
16	Dec	2	(h)	Coventry C	W	2-0	McCall, Watson	21,171
17		9	(a)	Tottenham H	L	1-2	Cottee	29,374
18		17	(h)	Manchester C	D	0-0		21,737
19		26	(a)	Derby Co	W	1-0	McCall	21,314
20		30	(a)	Q.P.R.	L	0-1		11,683
21	Jan	1	(h)	Luton T	W	2-1	Whiteside, Sharp	21,743
22		13	(a)	Southampton	D	2-2	Whiteside 2	19,381
23		20	(h)	Sheffield W	W	2-0	Sheedy 2	25,545
24	Feb	3	(a)	Liverpool	L	1-2	Sharp	38,370
25		10	(h)	Charlton Ath	W	2-1	Cottee, Whiteside	21,442
26	Mar	3	(a)	Wimbledon	L	1-3	Sheedy	6,512
27		14	(a)	Manchester U	D	0-0		37,398
28		17	(h)	Crystal Palace	W	4-0	Sharp, Cottee 2, Whiteside	19,274
29		21	(a)	Millwall	W	2-1	Pointon, Cottee	11,495
30		24	(h)	Norwich C	W	3-1	Cottee 2, Sharp	21,707
31		31	(a)	Arsenal	L	0-1		35,223
32	Apr	4	(h)	Nottingham F	W	4-0	Cottee 2, Whiteside 2	17,795
33		7	(h)	Q.P.R.	W	1-0	Cottee (pen)	19,887
34		14	(a)	Luton T	D	2-2	Cottee, Sharp	9,538
35		16	(h)	Derby Co	W	2-1	Atteveld, Sharp	23,933
36		21	(a)	Manchester C	L	0-1		32,144
37		28	(a)	Chelsea	L	1-2	Nevin	18,879
38	May	5	(h)	Aston Villa	D	3-3	Cascarino (og), Newell, Sheedy (pen)	29,551

FINAL LEAGUE POSITION : 6th in Division One

Appearances

Sub. Appearances

Goals

Southall	Snodin	Pointon	Ratcliffe	Watson	Whiteside	Nevin	McCall	Sharp	Newell	Sheedy	Cottee	Ebbrell	Keown	McDonald	Rehn	Beagrie	Atteveld	Wright	
1	2	3	4	5	6	7	8	9	10*	11	12								1
1	2	3	4	5	6	7	8	9	10	11									2
1	2	3	4	5	6	7	8	9*	10	11		12							3
1	2	3	4	5*	6	7	8		9	11	10†		12	14					4
1	2	3	4	5	6*	7	8	9	10	11				12					5
1	2	3	4	5		7*	8	9	10	11				12	6				6
1	2	3*	4	5	6†	7	8	9	10	11				12	14				7
1	2		4	5	6*	7	8	9	10	11				3	12				8
1	2†			5	6	7		12	9	11	10	8	4	3	14*				9
1				5	6	7	8		9	11	10	2	4	3					10
1				5	6	7	8		9	11	10	2	4	3					11
1				5†	6*	7	8	12	9	11	10	2	4	3		14			12
1		3			7	8	12	9	11	10*	2	4	5			6			13
1	7	3					8	9	10	11	2	4	5			6			14
1	6	3†		5		8	9	10	11	12	14	4		2		7*			15
1			4	5		8	9		11	10	6			3		7	2		16
1			4	5		8	9	12	11	10	6*			3		7	2		17
1			4	5		8	9	12	11	10	6*			3		7	2		18
1	2		4	5		14	8	9	12	11	10*			3		7	6†		19
1	2		4	5		14	8	9	12	11	10*			3		7	6†		20
1	2		4	5	6	7	8	9	10					3		11*	12		21
1	2		4		6	12	8	9	10	11			5	3		7*			22
1	2		4		6	7	8	9	10	11			5	3					23
1	2		4	5	6	7*	8	9	12	11			10	3					24
1	2		4	12	6	7	8	9		11	10		5	3*					25
1	2		4	5	12		8	9	14	11	10†		7	3*		6			26
1	2	3	4		6		8	9		11*	10			5		12	7		27
1	2	3	4		6	12	8	9		11	10			5			7*		28
1	2	3	4		6		8	9		11	10			5		12	7*		29
1	2	3	4†		6	14	8	9		11*	10			5		12	7		30
1	2	3		5	6	7	8	9		11*	10		4†	14		12			31
1	2†	3*		5	6	14	8	9		12	10			4		11	7		32
1				6	7*	8	9		12	10	3		4			11	2	5	33
1				5		7	8	9		6	10	3		4		11	2		34
1				5	6	7	8	9		12	10	3		4		11*	2		35
1		3		5	6	7	8	9*		11	10	12		4			2		36
1		3		5	6†	14	8		9	11	10	12	4	2		7*			37
1		3	4	5†		7	8		9	12	10	11*	2	6			14		38
38	25	19	24	28	26	23	37	30	20	33	25	13	19	26	1	14	16	1	
				1	1	7		3	6	4	2	4	1	5	3	5	2		
		1		1	9	4	3	6	7	9	13			1			1		

1990-91

1	Aug	25	(h)	Leeds U	L	2-3	Nevin, Ebbrell	34,412
2		29	(a)	Coventry C	L	1-3	Nevin	12,902
3	Sep	1	(a)	Manchester C	L	0-1		31,456
4		8	(h)	Arsenal	D	1-1	Newell	29,919
5		15	(a)	Sunderland	D	2-2	Sharp, Newell	25,004
6		22	(h)	Liverpool	L	2-3	Hinchcliffe, McCall	39,847
7		29	(h)	Southampton	W	3-0	Cottee 2, Ebbrell	23,093
8	Oct	7	(a)	Nottingham F	L	1-3	McDonald	25,790
9		20	(h)	Crystal Palace	D	0-0		24,504
10		27	(a)	Luton T	D	1-1	Nevin	10,047
11	Nov	3	(h)	Q.P.R.	W	3-0	Newell, Nevin, McDonald	22,352
12		10	(a)	Sheffield U	D	0-0		21,447
13		18	(h)	Tottenham H	D	1-1	McCall	28,716
14		24	(a)	Wimbledon	L	1-2	Sheedy (pen)	6,411
15	Dec	1	(h)	Manchester U	L	0-1		32,400
16		8	(h)	Coventry C	W	1-0	McCall	17,472
17		16	(a)	Leeds U	L	0-2		27,775
18		22	(a)	Norwich C	L	0-1		14,294
19		26	(h)	Aston Villa	W	1-0	Sharp	27,804
20		29	(h)	Derby Co	W	2-0	Newell, Nevin	25,361
21	Jan	1	(a)	Chelsea	W	2-1	Sharp, Cundy (og)	18,351
22		13	(h)	Manchester C	W	2-0	Beagrie, Sheedy	22,774
23		19	(a)	Arsenal	L	0-1		35,349
24	Feb	2	(h)	Sunderland	W	2-0	Sheedy, Beagrie	23,124
25		9	(a)	Liverpool	L	1-3	Nevin	25,116
26		23	(h)	Sheffield U	L	1-2	Cottee	28,148
27	Mar	2	(a)	Manchester U	W	2-0	Newell, Watson	45,656
28		16	(a)	Southampton	W	4-3	Watson, Milligan, Newell, Cottee	15,410
29		23	(h)	Nottingham F	D	0-0		23,078
30		30	(a)	Aston Villa	D	2-2	Warzycha 2	27,660
31	Apr	1	(h)	Norwich C	W	1-0	Newell	20,485
32		10	(h)	Wimbledon	L	1-2	Cottee	14,590
33		13	(h)	Chelsea	D	2-2	Cottee, Ebbrell	19,526
34		20	(a)	Crystal Palace	D	0-0		16,439
35		24	(a)	Tottenham H	D	3-3	Nevin, Stewart (og), Cottee	21,675
36	May	4	(h)	Luton T	W	1-0	Cottee	19,809
37		8	(a)	Derby Co	W	3-2	Cottee 2, Sheedy	12,403
38		11	(a)	Q.P.R.	D	1-1	Nevin	12,508

FINAL LEAGUE POSITION: 9th in Division One

Appearances

Sub. Appearances

Goals

Southall	McDonald	Hinchcliffe	Keown	Watson	Milligan	Nevin	McCall	Sharp	Newell	Ebbrell	Sheedy	Atteveld	Ratcliffe	Whiteside	Cottee	Beagrie	Snodin	Youds	Warzycha	Barlow	Jenkins	
1	2	3	4	5	6	7	8*	9	10	11	12											1
1	2*	3	4	5	8	7		9	10	6		11†	12	14								2
1		3	2	5	6	7		9	10	8	11*	12	4									3
1		3		5	6	7	8*	9	10	11		2	4		12							4
1		3		5	6	7	8	9	10	11		2	4									5
1	14	3		5	6†	7	8	9	10*	11		2	4		12							6
1	6	3		5		7	8	9*	12	11		2	4		10							7
1	6	3		5		7*	8	9	12	11		2	4		10							8
1	6	3†	14	5		7	8	9	12	11		2	4*		10							9
1	6	3		5		7	8	9		11		2	4		10							10
1	6	3		5		7	8	9	10			2	4			11						11
1	6	3		5		7	8	9		11	10*	2	4			12						12
1	6†		5			14	8	9	12	3	11	2	4		10	7*						13
1	2			5		14	8	9*	10	3	11	7	4	6†	12							14
1	2			5		7	8	12	9	3*	11	6	4		10							15
1	2	3		5	6	7	8	12	9	14	11†		4		10*							16
1	2	3		5	14		8	9†	10	6*	7		4		12	11						17
1	2	11	3†	5		7	12	9	6	8			4		10*			14				18
1	8	3	14	5		7*		9	12	6			4		10	11†		2				19
1	2	3		5		7	8	9	12	6	10		4			11*						20
1	2	3		5		7	8	9		6	10		4			11						21
1	2	3		5		7	8	9		6	10		4		12	11*						22
1	2	14	5†	6*		7	8	9		3	10		4		12	11						23
1	2		5	6*		7	8	9		3	10		4		12	11						24
1	2		5	6		7	8	9		3	10		4		12	11*						25
1	2	3	6	5		7	14	8	9*	12	11		4†		10							26
1	2	3	6	5		7†	8	9*	10	11		14	4		12							27
1	2		6	5	11	7*	8	9		3		14	4		10†	12						28
1	14	2	5†	6	11*	9	12	3		8			4		10				7			29
1	2	3		5	6	12	8	9		11*			4		10				7			30
1	2	3		5	6	12	8	9	14	11†					10			4	7*			31
1	2†	3		5	6*	9	8						4		10	11		14	7	12		32
1			4	5		7	8	9*		6	11		3		10		2			12		33
1			4	5†		7	8	9		6	11		3		10*	14	2	12				34
1		3		5		9	8			6	12		4		10	11	2*		7			35
1		3		5			8	9	2	6			4		10	11			7			36
1				5		9	8	12	3	6		2	4		10	11			7*			37
1			5†	12		7	8	9	2	6			4		10*	11		14			3	38
38	27	21	21	32	16	31	33	24	20	34	20	17	35	1	20	14	1	5	7	1		
	2		3		1	6		3	9	2	2	3	1	1		9	3		3	1	2	
	2	1		2	1	8	3	3	7	3	4				10	2			2			

1991-92

1	Aug	17	(a)	Nottingham F	L	1-2	Pearce (og)	24,422
2		20	(h)	Arsenal	W	3-1	Ward 2, Cottee	31,200
3		24	(h)	Manchester U	D	0-0		36,085
4		28	(a)	Sheffield W	L	1-2	Watson	28,690
5		31	(a)	Liverpool	L	1-3	Newell	39,072
6	Sep	3	(h)	Norwich C	D	1-1	Ward	19,197
7		7	(h)	Crystal Palace	D	2-2	Warzycha, Beardsley	21,065
8		14	(a)	Sheffield U	L	1-2	Beardsley	19,817
9		17	(a)	Manchester C	W	1-0	Beardsley	27,509
10		21	(h)	Coventry C	W	3-0	Beardsley 3 (1 pen)	20,542
11		28	(a)	Chelsea	D	2-2	Ebbrell, Beardsley	19,038
12	Oct	5	(h)	Tottenham H	W	3-1	Cottee 3 (1 pen)	29,505
13		19	(h)	Aston Villa	L	0-2		27,688
14		26	(a)	Q.P.R.	L	1-3	Cottee	10,002
15	Nov	2	(a)	Luton T	W	1-0	Warzycha	8,022
16		16	(h)	Wimbledon	W	2-0	Cottee (pen), Watson	18,762
17		23	(h)	Notts Co	W	1-0	Cottee	24,230
18		30	(a)	Leeds U	L	0-1		30,043
19	Dec	7	(h)	West Ham U	W	4-0	Cottee, Beagrie, Beardsley, Johnston	21,563
20		14	(a)	Oldham Ath	D	2-2	Sheedy, Nevin	14,955
21		21	(a)	Arsenal	L	2-4	Warzycha, Johnston	29,684
22		26	(h)	Sheffield W	L	0-1		30,788
23		28	(h)	Liverpool	D	1-1	Johnston	37,681
24	Jan	1	(a)	Southampton	W	2-1	Ward, Beardsley	16,546
25		11	(a)	Manchester U	L	0-1		46,619
26		19	(h)	Nottingham F	D	1-1	Watson	17,717
27	Feb	2	(a)	Aston Villa	D	0-0		17,451
28		8	(h)	Q.P.R.	D	0-0		18,212
29		23	(h)	Leeds U	D	1-1	Jackson	19,248
30		29	(a)	West Ham U	W	2-0	Johnston, Ablett	20,976
31	Mar	7	(h)	Oldham Ath	W	2-1	Beardsley 2	21,014
32		10	(a)	Wimbledon	D	0-0		3,569
33		14	(h)	Luton T	D	1-1	Johnston	16,707
34		17	(a)	Notts Co	D	0-0		7,480
35		21	(a)	Norwich C	L	3-4	Johnston 2, Beardsley	11,900
36	Apr	1	(h)	Southampton	L	0-1		15,201
37		4	(a)	Crystal Palace	L	0-2		14,338
38		11	(h)	Sheffield U	L	0-2		18,285
39		18	(a)	Coventry C	W	1-0	Beagrie	14,669
40		20	(h)	Manchester C	L	1-2	Nevin	21,101
41		25	(a)	Tottenham H	D	3-3	Beardsley 2, Unsworth	34,630
42	May	2	(h)	Chelsea	W	2-1	Beardsley (pen), Beagrie	20,163

FINAL LEAGUE POSITION: 13th in Division One

Appearances

Sub. Appearances

Goals

Southall	Harper	Ebbrell	Ratcliffe	Watson	Keown	Warzycha	Sheedy	Beardsley	Cottee	Ward	McDonald	Nevin	Newell	Hinchcliffe	Atteveld	Jackson	Beagrie	Johnston	Ablett	Barlow	Jenkins	Unsworth	
1	2	3	4	5	6	7†	8	9	10	11*	12	14											1
1	2	3	4	5	6	7	8	9	10	11*		12											2
1	2	3	4	5	6	7*	8	9	10†	11		12	14										3
1	2	3	4	5	6	7*	8	9	10†	11	12		14										4
1	2	3	12	5	6*	14	11	8	10†	7	4	9											5
1	2	6	4	5		7	10	8		11		9	3										6
1	2†	3	4	5	6	7*	10	8		11	12	9	14										7
1		4		5	6	7	10	8	12	11*		9	3	2									8
1		4		5	6	7*	10	8	11	12		9	3	2									9
1		4		5	6	7	10*	8	11	12		9	3	2									10
1		4		5	6	7*	10	8	12		11	9	3	2									11
1	2	4	3	5	6	7	10†	8	9	11*		12	14										12
1	10	4	3*	5	6	7	11†	8	9		12	14	2										13
1		4		5	6	7*	10	8	9	11†		12	3	14	2								14
1		4		5	6	14		8	12		7*	9	3	10	2†	11							15
1	10	4		5	6			8	9	7				3		2	11						16
1	14	4		5	6	12		8	10	7				3		2	11*	9†					17
1	3	4		5	6	12		8	10	7*						9	2	11					18
1		4		5	6	12		8	10	7*				3		2	11	9					19
1	12	4		5	6	7†	10*	8				14		3		2	11	9					20
1	3	4		5		7	10*	8	12			14				2	6	11†	9				21
1	3	4		5	6	7*		8	10	11						2	12	9					22
1	3	4		5	6	7*		8	10	12						2	11	9					23
1	3	4		5	6	7*		8	10	12					14	2	11†	9					24
1	3	4		5	6	7†		8	12	10					14	2	11*	9					25
1	10	4		5	6	7*		8	12	11						2†	14	9	3				26
1		4		5	6		8*		10	11		7				2	9		3				27
1	10*	4		5	6	12		8		7		14				2	11	9†	3				28
1		4		5	6	7†		8	10*	11		14				2	12	9	3				29
1	14	4		5	6			8	10†	7		11				2*	12	9	3				30
1	10	4		5	6*			8		7		11				2	12	9	3				31
1	14	4		5	6	10†		8		7		11				2	12	9*	3				32
1	10	4		5	6	12		8		7		14				2†	11	9*	3				33
1	10	4	5†	6		12		8		7		11*				2	14	9	3				34
1	10	4			6	7		8		11				5		2		9	3*	12			35
1	3	4			6	7*		8	12	10						2	11	9	5				36
1	3	4			6	7*		8		10						2	11	9	5	12			37
1	2	4			6*			8	10†	7		14				5	11	9	3	12			38
1	10			5	6			8		4		7				2	11	9*	3	12			39
1	3	4			6	12		8		10		7*				2†	11		5	9	14		40
1	4							2		8		10				6	11		5	9	3*	12	41
1	4†				6	12		8		10		7				2	11		5	9*	14	3	42
42	29	39	8	35	39	26	16	42	17	37	1	7	8	15	8	30	20	21	17	3	1	1	
	4		1		11		7		4	10	5	3	5		7			4	2	1			
		1		3		3	1	15	8	4		2	1			1	3	7	1		1		

49

1992-93

1	Aug	15	(h)	Sheffield W	D	1-1	Horne	27,687
2		19	(a)	Manchester U	W	3-0	Beardsley, Warzycha, Johnston	31,901
3		22	(a)	Norwich C	D	1-1	Beardsley	14,150
4		25	(h)	Aston Villa	W	1-0	Johnston	22,372
5		29	(h)	Wimbledon	D	0-0		18,118
6	Sep	5	(a)	Tottenham H	L	1-2	Beardsley	26,503
7		12	(h)	Manchester U	L	0-2		30,002
8		15	(a)	Blackburn R	W	3-2	Cottee 2, Ebbrell	19,563
9		19	(h)	Crystal Palace	L	0-2		18,080
10		26	(a)	Leeds U	L	0-2		27,915
11	Oct	4	(a)	Oldham Ath	L	0-1		13,013
12		17	(h)	Coventry C	D	1-1	Beagrie	17,587
13		24	(a)	Arsenal	L	0-2		28,052
14		31	(h)	Manchester C	L	1-3	Brightwell (og)	20,242
15	Nov	7	(a)	Nottingham F	W	1-0	Rideout	20,941
16		21	(h)	Chelsea	L	0-1		17,418
17		28	(a)	Ipswich T	L	0-1		18,034
18	Dec	7	(h)	Liverpool	W	2-1	Johnston, Beardsley	35,826
19		12	(a)	Sheffield U	L	0-1		16,266
20		19	(h)	Southampton	W	2-1	Beardsley (pen), Rideout	14,051
21		26	(h)	Middlesbrough	D	2-2	Rideout, Beardsley (pen)	24,391
22		28	(a)	Q.P.R.	L	2-4	Barlow 2	14,802
23	Jan	9	(a)	Crystal Palace	W	2-0	Jackson, Beardsley	13,227
24		16	(h)	Leeds U	W	2-0	Cottee 2	21,031
25		26	(a)	Wimbledon	W	3-1	Cottee 2, Snodin	3,039
26		30	(h)	Norwich C	L	0-1		20,301
27	Feb	6	(a)	Sheffield W	L	1-3	Cottee	24,979
28		10	(h)	Tottenham H	L	1-2	Sansom	16,164
29		20	(a)	Aston Villa	L	1-2	Beardsley (pen)	32,913
30		27	(h)	Oldham Ath	D	2-2	Beardsley (pen), Barlow	18,025
31	Mar	3	(h)	Blackburn R	W	2-1	Hendry (og), Cottee	18,086
32		7	(a)	Coventry C	W	1-0	Ward	11,285
33		10	(a)	Chelsea	L	1-2	Kenny	12,739
34		13	(h)	Nottingham F	W	3-0	Cottee 2, Hinchcliffe	21,271
35		20	(a)	Liverpool	L	0-1		44,619
36		24	(h)	Ipswich T	W	3-0	Barlow, Jackson, Cottee	15,638
37	Apr	10	(a)	Middlesbrough	W	2-1	Watson, Radosavljevic	16,627
38		12	(h)	Q.P.R.	L	3-5	Cottee, Barlow, Radosavljevic	19,057
39		17	(a)	Southampton	D	0-0		16,911
40	May	1	(h)	Arsenal	D	0-0		19,044
41		4	(h)	Sheffield U	L	0-2		15,197
42		8	(a)	Manchester C	W	5-2	Jackson, Beagrie 2, Beardsley, Radosavljevic	25,180

FINAL LEAGUE POSITION: 13th in Premier League

Appearances

Sub. Appearances

Goals

Southall	Jackson	Hinchcliffe	Ebbrell	Watson	Ablett	Ward	Beardsley	Rideout	Horne	Beagrie	Warzycha	Harper	Johnston	Barlow	Cottee	Unsworth	Radosavljevic	Keown	Kenny	Snodin	Jenkins	Kearton	Sansom	Holmes	Moore	
1	2	3	4	5	6	7	8	9	10*	11	12															1
1		3	4	5	6	11	8	9*	10	12	7†	2	14													2
1		3	4†	5	6	11	8	9	10	12	7*	2	14													3
1		3	4	5	6	7	8	9*	10	12		2	11													4
1		3	4	5	6	11*	8	9†	10	12	7	2	14													5
1		3	4	5	6	11	8		10	12	7*	2	9†	14												6
1		3	4*	5	6	11	8		10	12	7	2	9													7
1	14	3	11	5	6	7*	8	9†	4		12	2			10											8
1	12	3	4	5	6		8*	9†	11	7		2	14		10											9
1		3	4	5	6				8	12	7†	2	14		10	9*	11									10
1		3	4	5	6			9	8	12	7	2	10†		14		11*									11
1		3		5	6		8		10*	11	2†				9	14		4	7	12						12
1		3*		5	6		8	12	10	11	7		14		9			4		2†						13
1	2			5	3			9	10*	11	7			8			12	6	4							14
1	2	11		5	3		8	9	10	12	7*							6	4							15
1	2	11		5	3		8	9	10†	12	7*		14					6	4							16
1		11		5	3		8	12				2	14	10†	9			6	7	4*						17
1				5	3		8	14			12	2		10	9	11*		6	7	4†						18
1	2†			5	3		8	14		12	7		10*		9	11		6	4							19
1				5	3		8	9	4	11	7							6	10	2						20
1				5	3		8	9	4	11	7†			14		3	12	10	2*							21
1				5	3		8	9	4	11†	7*		14				12	6	10	2						22
1	2	11		5	3		8	9*									12	7	6	10	4					23
1	2		4	5	3		8		10	11†			14		9*		12	7	6							24
1	2			5	3		8		10						9	11*	12	6	4							25
1	2			5	6		8	14	10		7				9	7†	12	11	4†							26
1	2			5	6		8				7*		3		9	11†	12	10	4				14	3		27
1	4			5	6		8		10	11					9		12	7*						3		28
	2			5	6		8		11		7†	2†	14	14	9		12	4					1	3		29
	2			5	6		8	12	10			10*	11*		9		7	4					1	3		30
1	2	11		5	6	7	8		10						9		12	4*						3		31
1	2	11		5	6	7	8		10						9		12	4*						3		32
1	2	3		5	6	7	8			11					9		12	4*								33
1	2	3		5	6	7	8						12		9		11†	4*	10				14			34
1	2	3	11	5	6	7	8							14	9		12	10†	4							35
1	6	3	10	5		7†	8	14		12					11		9	4*					2			36
1	2	3	11	5	6	7	8	10†	4						14*		9	12						3		37
1	2†	3	11	5	6	7*	8		4						14		9	12	10							38
1	6	3	4	5		11	8								10*		9	7	12				2			39
1	2	3	10	5	6	11*	8								9		12	4	7							40
1	5	3	4		6		8	10†		11					12		9	7*					2	14		41
1†	5	3	4		6		8			11					12		9	10*					14	2		42
40	25	25	24	40	40	19	39	17	34	11	15	16	7	8	25	3	13	13	16	19	1	2	6	4		
	2							7		11	5	2	6	18	1			10	1	1			3	1	1	
		3	1	1	1		1	10	3	1	3	1	3	5	12			3	1	1				1		

1993-94

1	Aug	14	(a)	Southampton	W	2-0	Beagrie, Ebbrell	14,051
2		17	(h)	Manchester C	W	1-0	Rideout	26,025
3		21	(h)	Sheffield U	W	4-2	Cottee 3, Ebbrell	24,177
4		25	(a)	Newcastle U	L	0-1		34,490
5		28	(a)	Arsenal	L	0-2		29,063
6		31	(h)	Aston Villa	L	0-1		24,067
7	Sep	11	(a)	Oldham Ath	W	1-0	Cottee	13,666
8		18	(h)	Liverpool	W	2-0	Ward, Cottee	38,157
9		25	(h)	Norwich C	L	1-5	Rideout	20,631
10	Oct	3	(a)	Tottenham H	L	2-3	Rideout, Cottee (pen)	27,487
11		16	(a)	Swindon T	D	1-1	Beagrie	14,437
12		23	(h)	Manchester U	L	0-1		35,455
13		30	(a)	Ipswich T	W	2-0	Barlow, Whelan (og)	15,078
14	Nov	6	(a)	Coventry C	L	1-2	Rideout	11,550
15		20	(h)	Q.P.R.	L	0-3		17,326
16		23	(h)	Leeds U	D	1-1	Cottee	17,102
17		27	(a)	Wimbledon	D	1-1	Barlow	6,934
18	Dec	4	(h)	Southampton	W	1-0	Cottee	13,265
19		8	(a)	Manchester C	L	0-1		20,513
20		11	(a)	Sheffield U	D	0-0		15,135
21		18	(h)	Newcastle U	L	0-2		25,362
22		27	(h)	Sheffield W	L	0-2		16,471
23		29	(a)	Blackburn R	L	0-2		22,061
24	Jan	1	(h)	West Ham U	L	0-1		19,602
25		3	(a)	Chelsea	L	2-4	Cottee, Barlow	18,338
26		15	(h)	Swindon T	W	6-2	Ebbrell, Cottee 3 (1 pen), Ablett, Beagrie	20,760
27		22	(a)	Manchester U	L	0-1		44,750
28	Feb	5	(h)	Chelsea	W	4-2	Ebbrell, Rideout 2, Angell	18,201
29		12	(h)	Ipswich T	D	0-0		19,641
30		19	(h)	Arsenal	D	1-1	Cottee	19,760
31	Mar	5	(h)	Oldham Ath	W	2-1	Radosavljevic, Stuart	18,881
32		13	(a)	Liverpool	L	1-2	Watson	44,281
33		21	(a)	Norwich C	L	0-3		16,432
34		26	(h)	Tottenham H	L	0-1		23,460
35		29	(a)	Aston Villa	D	0-0		36,044
36	Apr	2	(a)	Sheffield W	L	1-5	Cottee	24,080
37		4	(h)	Blackburn R	L	0-3		27,463
38		9	(a)	West Ham U	W	1-0	Cottee	20,243
39		16	(a)	Q.P.R.	L	1-2	Cottee	13,330
40		23	(h)	Coventry C	D	0-0		23,352
41		30	(a)	Leeds U	L	0-3		35,487
42	May	7	(h)	Wimbledon	W	3-2	Stuart 2 (1 pen), Horne	31,233

FINAL LEAGUE POSITION: 17th in Premiership

Appearances

Sub. Appearances

Goals

Southall	Holmes	Jackson	Snodin	Watson	Ablett	Ward	Ebbrell	Cottee	Rideout	Beagrie	Radosavljevic	Barlow	Hinchcliffe	Stuart	Horne	Angell	Warzycha	Unsworth	Moore	Limpar	Rowett	
1	2	3	4	5	6	7	8	9	10	11												1
1	2	3	4*	5†	6	7	8	9	10	11	12	14										2
1	2	5			6	7	4	9	10	11*	12	14	3	8†								3
1	2†	5			6	7	4	9	10	11*	12	14	3	8								4
1	2	5			6	7	4	9†	10		12	14	3	8*	11							5
1		5			6	7	4	9	10†	11	12	14	3	8*	2							6
1	2	5			6	7	4	9	10†	11	8*	14	3		12							7
1	2	5			6	7	4	9	10	11*	12		3	8								8
1	2†	5			6	7*	4	9	10	11	12		3	8		14						9
1	2	5			6	7	4	9†	10	11*	12	14	3	8								10
1	2	5			6	7	4	9	10†	11	12	14*	3	8								11
1	2	14	5		6	7†	4	9		11	12	10*	3	8								12
1	2	12	5		6	7	4	9		11*		10	3	8								13
1	2			5	6	7*	4	9	10	11		12	3	8								14
1	2	3		5	6	7	4	9		11†	8*	10		14	12							15
1		2	11†	5	6	7	4	9		10*	12		3	14	8							16
1		2	11	5	6	7	4	9			12	10†	3	14	8*							17
1	2	6	5	3		7*	4	9		11				10	8		12					18
1	2	6	5	3		7	4	9		11				10	8*		12					19
1	2	6	5	3		7	4	9		11					8			10				20
1	2	6	5	3		7	4	9			12	10		8			11*					21
1	2	6	5*	3		7	4			11	12†	10		9	8	14						22
1	5	2			6	7	4	9		11			3	8	10		12	10*				23
1	2	5	3		6	7†	4	9*	10	11		12		14	8							24
1	2	5†	6		3	7		9	10*	11		12		8	4		14					25
1	5	2			6	7	4	9*		11	12		3	8	10							26
1	2	6		3			4	9*		11	12	14		8	10	7†		5				27
1	2	5			6		4	9		11	7		3	8	10							28
1	2	6	14			4	12	9*		11	7†		3	8	10				5			29
1	2	4	5				12	9*		11	7†		3	8	14	10			6			30
1	2	6	5		14			9	12	11	7†		3	8	4	10*						31
1	2	6	5				4	9	12	11	7†		3	8	14	10*						32
1	2	6	5				4	9	10	11	7*		3	8	12							33
1	2	6	5				4	9	10*				3	7	8	12				11		34
1	2	6	5				4						3	7	8	10		9		11		35
1	2	6	5				4	12					7	8	10†	3		9*		11	14	36
1	2	6	5				4	9			12		7	8	10*			3		11		37
1	2	3	5	6		4	9	12					7	8	10*					11		38
1	2	3	5	6		4	9						7	8	10					11		39
1	2					4	9				12		3	7	8*	10		6		11		40
1			3	5	6	4	9	10					7	8			2			11*	12	41
1			3	5	6	4*	9	10			12		7	8			2			11		42
42	15	37	28	27	32	26	39	36	21	29	9	6	25	26	28	13	3	7	4	9		
	1	1	1		1			3	3		14	16	1	4	4	3	4	1		2		
				1	1	1	4	16	6	3	1	3	3	1	1							

53

1994-95

#				Opponent		Score	Scorers	Attendance
1	Aug	20	(h)	Aston Villa	D	2-2	Stuart, Rideout	35,552
2		24	(a)	Tottenham H	L	1-2	Rideout	24,553
3		27	(a)	Manchester C	L	0-4		19,867
4		30	(h)	Nottingham F	L	1-2	Rideout	26,689
5	Sep	10	(a)	Blackburn R	L	0-3		26,548
6		17	(h)	Q.P.R.	D	2-2	Amokachi, Rideout	27,291
7		24	(h)	Leicester C	D	1-1	Ablett	28,015
8	Oct	1	(a)	Manchester U	L	0-2		43,803
9		8	(a)	Southampton	L	0-2		15,163
10		15	(h)	Coventry C	L	0-2		28,219
11		22	(a)	Crystal Palace	L	0-1		15,026
12		29	(h)	Arsenal	D	1-1	Unsworth	32,005
13	Nov	1	(h)	West Ham U	W	1-0	Ablett	28,353
14		5	(a)	Norwich C	D	0-0		18,377
15		21	(h)	Liverpool	W	2-0	Ferguson, Rideout	39,866
16		26	(a)	Chelsea	W	1-0	Rideout	28,115
17	Dec	5	(h)	Leeds U	W	3-0	Rideout, Ferguson, Unsworth (pen)	25,906
18		10	(a)	Aston Villa	D	0-0		29,678
19		17	(h)	Tottenham H	D	0-0		32,813
20		26	(h)	Sheffield W	L	1-4	Ferguson	37,089
21		31	(h)	Ipswich T	W	4-1	Ferguson, Rideout 2, Watson	25,667
22	Jan	2	(a)	Wimbledon	L	1-2	Rideout	9,506
23		14	(a)	Arsenal	D	1-1	Watson	34,743
24		21	(h)	Crystal Palace	W	3-1	Ferguson 2, Rideout	23,734
25		24	(a)	Liverpool	D	0-0		39,505
26	Feb	1	(a)	Newcastle U	L	0-2		34,465
27		4	(h)	Norwich C	W	2-1	Stuart, Rideout	23,295
28		13	(a)	West Ham U	D	2-2	Rideout, Limpar	21,081
29		22	(a)	Leeds U	L	0-1		30,793
30		25	(h)	Manchester U	W	1-0	Ferguson	40,011
31	Mar	4	(a)	Leicester C	D	2-2	Limpar, Samways	20,447
32		8	(a)	Nottingham F	L	1-2	Barlow	24,526
33		15	(h)	Manchester C	D	1-1	Unsworth (pen)	28,485
34		18	(a)	Q.P.R.	W	3-2	Barlow, McDonald (og), Hinchcliffe	14,488
35	Apr	1	(h)	Blackburn R	L	1-2	Stuart	37,905
36		14	(h)	Newcastle U	W	2-0	Amokachi 2	34,628
37		17	(a)	Sheffield W	D	0-0		27,880
38		29	(h)	Wimbledon	D	0-0		31,567
39	May	3	(h)	Chelsea	D	3-3	Hinchcliffe, Ablett, Amokachi	33,180
40		6	(h)	Southampton	D	0-0		36,851
41		9	(a)	Ipswich T	W	1-0	Rideout	14,940
42		14	(a)	Coventry C	D	0-0		21,787

FINAL LEAGUE POSITION: 15th in F.A. Carling Premiership

Appearances

Sub. Appearances

Goals

Football appearance/scoring grid (squad positions per match). Columns are players; rows are matches 1–42; the final three rows are appearance totals, substitute appearances, and goals.

Southall	Jackson	Ablett	Ebbrell	Watson	Unsworth	Samways	Stuart	Cottee	Rideout	Limpar	Parkinson	Angell	Hinchcliffe	Burrows	Amokachi	Snodin	Holmes	Rowett	Barlow	Durrant	Ferguson	Horne	Kearton	Grant	Barrett	#
1	2	3	4	5*	6	7	8	9	10	11	12															1
1	2	3	4	5	6	7	8	9	10*	11†	12	14														2
1	2	3	4	5	6	7	8	9*	10	12	11															3
1	2		4	5	6	7	8		10	11		9	3													4
1	2		4	5	6	7	8		10	11			3	9												5
1	2		4	5	6	7	8		10	11*			3	9	12											6
1		4		5	6	7	8					10	3	9	11	2										7
1				5	6	7	8*				4		11	3	9	2		10	12							8
1	2*		5†	6	7		12		10		4		11	3	9		8			14						9
1	2	5		6	7		12			4*			3		9				11		10	8				10
1	2	5		6	7*		8			12			3		9				11		10	4				11
1	2	5		6*			8		12	14	4		3		9				11†		10	7				12
1	2	6		5			8†		12	14	4		3		9*				11		10	7				13
1	2	4		5	6*		8		10	12	11										9	7				14
1	2*	3	4	5	6	12	8		14	11					9†						10	7				15
1	2		4	5	6				10	11	8		3								9	7				16
1	2	3*	4	5	6	12			10		8		11								9	7				17
	2		4	5	6				10	7	8		11	3							9		1			18
1	2		4	5	6				10	12	8*		11	3							9	7				19
1	2		4	5	6	7			10	12			11	3*							9	8				20
1	2		4	5	6				10		8		11	3							9	7				21
1	2		4	5	6				10		8		11	3*					12		9	7				22
1	2		4	5	6				10		8		11	3							9	7				23
1	2		4	5	6				10		8		11	3							9	7				24
1	2		4	5	6				10		8		11	3							9	7				25
1	2		4	5	6	12	9		7†	10				11*							8			14	3	26
1		3	4	5	6	12	9		10	8*			11									7			2	27
1	3*	4	5	6			8		10	12			11								9	7			2	28
1	6	4	5			12			10*	11	8		3								9	7			2	29
1		4*	5	6		12				11	8		3							10	9	7			2	30
1	12		5	6	7				14	11†	4		3							10*	9	8			2	31
1	3		5	6	7	12				11	4*									10	9	8			2	32
1	6†	4	5			12			14	11	8*		3							10	9	7			2	33
1	12	6	4	5						11	10†		3	14							9	7		8*	2	34
1	2	6	5				8			11			3		9				10*		12	7			4	35
1		3	5	6			8			7	4		11		9*						12	10			2	36
1	12	3	5	6					10	7	4	*	11*								9†	8		14	2	37
1		3	5	6		12			10	7*	4		11								9	8			2	38
1		3	5	6		8*			10		4		11						12		9	7			2	39
1		3	4*	5	6	12			10	14	8		11†								9	7			2	40
1		3	4	5	6	12			10	7*			11		9†					14		8			2	41
1	5	3	4		6	7*	8		10	11					9							12			2	42
41	26	26	26	38	37	14	20	3	25	19	32	3	28	19	17	2	1	2	7	4	22	31	1	1	17	
	3			1	5	8	4	8	2	1	1		1	1					4	1	1	4				
		3		2	3	1	3		14	2			2		4						2				7	

55

1995-96

1	Aug	19	(a)	Chelsea	D	0-0		30,189
2		23	(h)	Arsenal	L	0-2		36,047
3		26	(h)	Southampton	W	2-0	Limpar, Amokachi	33,676
4		30	(a)	Manchester C	W	2-0	Parkinson, Amokachi	28,432
5	Sep	9	(h)	Manchester U	L	2-3	Limpar, Rideout	39,496
6		17	(a)	Nottingham F	L	2-3	Rideout 2	24,786
7		23	(a)	West Ham U	L	1-2	Samways	21,085
8	Oct	1	(h)	Newcastle U	L	1-3	Limpar	33,026
9		14	(a)	Bolton W	D	1-1	Rideout	20,427
10		22	(h)	Tottenham H	D	1-1	Stuart	33,629
11		28	(a)	Aston Villa	L	0-1		32,792
12	Nov	5	(h)	Blackburn R	W	1-0	Stuart	30,097
13		18	(a)	Liverpool	W	2-1	Kanchelskis 2	40,818
14		22	(h)	Q.P.R.	W	2-0	Stuart, Rideout	30,009
15		25	(h)	Sheffield W	D	2-2	Kanchelskis, Amokachi	35,898
16	Dec	2	(a)	Tottenham H	D	0-0		32,894
17		11	(h)	West Ham U	W	3-0	Stuart, Unsworth (pen), Ebbrell	31,778
18		16	(a)	Newcastle U	L	0-1		36,557
19		23	(a)	Coventry C	L	1-2	Rideout	16,638
20		26	(h)	Middlesbrough	W	4-0	Short, Stuart 2, Kanchelskis	40,091
21		30	(h)	Leeds U	W	2-0	Wetherall (og), Kanchelskis	40,009
22	Jan	1	(a)	Wimbledon	W	3-2	Ebbrell, Ferguson 2	11,121
23		13	(h)	Chelsea	D	1-1	Unsworth (pen)	34,968
24		20	(a)	Arsenal	W	2-1	Stuart, Kanchelskis	38,275
25	Feb	3	(a)	Southampton	D	2-2	Stuart, Horne	15,126
26		10	(h)	Manchester C	W	2-0	Parkinson, Hinchcliffe (pen)	37,354
27		21	(a)	Manchester U	L	0-2		42,459
28		24	(h)	Nottingham F	W	3-0	Kanchelskis, Watson, Ferguson	33,163
29	Mar	2	(a)	Middlesbrough	W	2-0	Grant, Hinchcliffe (pen)	29,805
30		9	(h)	Coventry C	D	2-2	Ferguson 2	34,517
31		17	(a)	Leeds U	D	2-2	Stuart, Kanchelskis	29,422
32		23	(a)	Wimbledon	L	2-4	Short, Kanchelskis	31,282
33		30	(a)	Blackburn R	W	3-0	Amokachi, Kanchelskis 2	29,468
34	Apr	6	(h)	Bolton W	W	3-0	Hottiger, Kanchelskis, Amokachi	37,974
35		8	(a)	Q.P.R.	L	1-3	Ebbrell	18,349
36		16	(h)	Liverpool	D	1-1	Kanchelskis	40,120
37		27	(a)	Sheffield W	W	5-2	Amokachi, Ebbrell, Kanchelskis 3	32,724
38	May	5	(h)	Aston Villa	W	1-0	Parkinson	40,127

FINAL LEAGUE POSITION: 6th in F.A. Carling Premiership

Appearances

Sub. Appearances

Goals

Southall	Barrett	Hinchcliffe	Unsworth	Watson	Ablett	Limpar	Horne	Ferguson	Rideout	Parkinson	Samways	Amokachi	Barlow	Kanchelskis	Holmes	Short	Grant	Stuart	Ebbrell	Jackson	O'Connor	Branch	Hottiger	
1	2	3	4	5	6	7*	8	9	10	11	12													1
1	2	3	4	5	6	7*	8	9	10	11†		12	13											2
1	2		4	5	3	11	8		10	6		9		7										3
1	2	12	4	5	3	11*	8		10	6		9		7										4
1		12	4	5	3	11	8		10	6		9		7*	2									5
1	2	11		5	3†	7*	8		10	4		9	12			6	13							6
1	2	3		5		12	8		10†	4	7	9				6	11*	13						7
1	2	3	4	5		12	7		10	11*						8	9	6						8
1	2	3			6*	12	8		10			9	13	7†		5		11	4					9
1		11*		5	3	12	8		10	4				7		6		9		2				10
1		3*	13	5	6	12			10	11		9†		7		8			4	2				11
1		3		5		11	8		10			12		7		6		9*	4	2				12
1		12		5	3*	11	8		10					7		6		9	4	2				13
1		3		5		11	8		10					7		6		9	4	2				14
1		3	6	5		11	8		10*			12		7				9	4	2				15
1		12	3	5		11	8	9						7		6*		10	4	2				16
1		3		5		11*	8	9			12			7		6		10	4	2				17
1		3		5		11	12	13		8*		9		7		6		10	4	2†				18
1		3		5		11*	8	9			12			7		6		10	4	2				19
1		3		5		11	8		10	4				7		6		9		2				20
1		12	3	5			8	9*	10	4				7		6		11		2				21
1		12	3	5			8	9	10	4				7*				11	2		6			22
1		3*	4		6	11	8		10			12		7		5		9		2				23
1		12		5	3		8	9		4		10*		7		6		11	2					24
1		3		5		11*	8	9		4		12		7				10		2				25
1		11	3	5		7	8	9		4						6		10		2				26
1		3	6	5			8	9						7		11*		10	4		2	12		27
1		3	6	5				9*	8			12		7		11		10	4		2			28
1		3	6	5				9	8					7		11		10	4		2			29
1		3	6					9	8*			12		7		11	5†	10	4	13			2	30
1		3	6			11	8	9						7			5	10	4				2	31
1		3		5		11	8	9				12	13	7		6		10†	4*				2	32
1		3	4	5		11*	8	9	12†			13		7		6		10					2	33
1		3	6	5			8	9		4		10		7		11*		12					2	34
1		3	6*	5		11°	8†	9	10					7		12	13		4		14		2	35
1		3	6	5			8	9				10*		7		11		12	4				2	36
1		3		5		12		9						7		6	8	11	4		10*		2	37
1		3	6	5		12	8	9†		4		13		7		11*		10					2	38
38	8	23	28	34	13	22	25	16	19	28	3	17		32	1	22	11	27	24	14	3	1	9	
	5	3			6	1	2	6				1	8	3		1	2	2	1		1	2		
		2	2	1		3	1	5	6	3	1	6		16		2	1	9	4				1	

1996-97

1	Aug	17	(h)	Newcastle U	W	2-0	Unsworth (pen), Speed	40,117
2		21	(a)	Manchester U	D	2-2	Ferguson 2	54,943
3		24	(a)	Tottenham H	D	0-0		29,669
4	Sep	4	(h)	Aston Villa	L	0-1		39,115
5		7	(a)	Wimbledon	L	0-4		13,684
6		14	(h)	Middlesbrough	L	1-2	Short	39,250
7		21	(a)	Blackburn R	D	1-1	Unsworth	27,091
8		28	(h)	Sheffield W	W	2-0	Kanchelskis, Stuart	34,160
9	Oct	12	(h)	West Ham U	W	2-1	Stuart, Speed	36,541
10		28	(a)	Nottingham F	W	1-0	Short	19,892
11	Nov	4	(h)	Coventry C	D	1-1	Stuart (pen)	31,477
12		16	(h)	Southampton	W	7-1	Stuart, Kanchelskis 2, Speed 3, Barmby	35,669
13		20	(a)	Liverpool	D	1-1	Speed	40,751
14		23	(a)	Leicester C	W	2-1	Hinchcliffe, Unsworth	20,975
15		30	(h)	Sunderland	L	1-3	Ferguson	40,087
16	Dec	7	(a)	Chelsea	D	2-2	Branch, Kanchelskis	27,920
17		16	(a)	Derby Co	W	1-0	Barmby	17,252
18		21	(h)	Leeds U	D	0-0		36,954
19		26	(a)	Middlesbrough	L	2-4	Unsworth (pen), Ferguson	29,673
20		28	(h)	Wimbledon	L	1-3	Stuart	36,733
21	Jan	1	(h)	Blackburn R	L	0-2		30,427
22		11	(a)	Sheffield W	L	1-2	Ferguson	24,175
23		19	(a)	Arsenal	L	1-3	Ferguson	38,095
24		29	(a)	Newcastle U	L	1-4	Speed	36,143
25	Feb	1	(h)	Nottingham F	W	2-0	Ferguson, Barmby	32,567
26		22	(a)	Coventry C	D	0-0		19,452
27	Mar	1	(h)	Arsenal	L	0-2		36,980
28		5	(a)	Southampton	D	2-2	Ferguson, Speed	15,134
29		8	(a)	Leeds U	L	0-1		32,055
30		15	(h)	Derby Co	W	1-0	Watson	32,140
31		22	(h)	Manchester U	L	0-2		40,079
32	Apr	5	(a)	Aston Villa	L	1-3	Unsworth	39,339
33		9	(h)	Leicester C	D	1-1	Branch	30,368
34		12	(h)	Tottenham H	W	1-0	Speed	36,380
35		16	(h)	Liverpool	D	1-1	Ferguson	40,177
36		19	(a)	West Ham U	D	2-2	Branch, Ferguson	24,525
37	May	3	(a)	Sunderland	L	0-3		22,052
38		11	(h)	Chelsea	L	1-2	Barmby	38,321

FINAL LEAGUE POSITION: 15th in F.A. Carling Premiership

Appearances

Sub. Appearances

Goals

Southall	Barrett	Hinchcliffe	Unsworth	Watson	Parkinson	Kanchelskis	Stuart	Ferguson	Ebbrell	Speed	Short	Grant	Rideout	Branch	Limpar	Hottiger	Barmby	Gerrard	Allen	Hills	Phelan	Dunne	Thomsen	Ball	Cadamarteri	
1	2	3	4	5*	6	7	8	9	10	11	12															1
1	2	3	4		6	7*	8	9	10	11	5	12														2
1	2	3	4		6	7	8*	9		11	5	10	12													3
1	2	3	4		6	7	8*	9		11	5	10	12													4
1	2	3	4		6	7	8	9		11	5	10*	12													5
1	2	3	4		6	7	12	9	8	11	5	10*														6
1	2	3	4		6	7		9	8		5	12	10	11*												7
1	2	3	4		6	7	8		10	11	5		9													8
1	2	3	4		6*	7		9	8†	11	5	12	10	13												9
1	2	3	4	5	8	7		9		11	6	12	10*													10
1	2	3	4*	5	6†	7	8			11	10	13	12				9									11
1°	2	3	4	5	6	7	8			11	10						9	14								12
1	2	3	4	5	6	7*	8	12		11	10						9									13
1	2	3	4	5	6		8	9		11	12	10*					7									14
1	2	3†	4	5	6	7°	8	12		11	13	10*	14				9									15
1	2	3	4	5	6	7	12	9		11	10						8*									16
1	2	3	4	5	6	7	12	9		11	10*						8									17
1	2	3†	12	5	6	7		9		11	4*	10		13			8									18
1	2		4	5†	6	8	9	3		10	12			11*	14		7		13°							19
1	5		4		8	9	6†	3		11	10*	12				2	7			13						20
1	4	5		7*	10	9	6			11		13	12			2	8†			3						21
1	2	12	5	7	10†	9				11		13	4	14			8				3°	6*				22
1	2		4	5	7*	10	9			11	12						8			3		6				23
	2		4	5	8	7	9			11	6*	12†	13					1		3			10			24
	2		4	5	6	7	9			11							8	1		3			10			25
	2		4	5		7	9			11	6						8	1		3			10			26
1	2	4*	5	6	7		9			11	12	13					8†			3			10			27
1	2	4	5	8	12		9			11	6	13					7†			3			10*			28
1	2	4	5	8*	12		9			11	6°	14	13				7†			3			10			29
1	2	4	5	8	12		9				6			11*		13	7			3			10†			30
	2		4	5	6		8	9		11		12					7	1		3			10*			31
1		4†	5	8	7		9			11	6	12				2*				3		13	10			32
1		4	5	6†	7		9			11	2	10	12				8*			3		13				33
1	2		5		7		9			11	4		8*	12							3†	6	10	13		34
1	2	3	5		7		9			11	4†	12					8					6	10*		13	35
1	2	3	5		7		9			11		12					8					6	10	4*		36
1	2		5		7†		9			11	10	12					8				3*	6		4	13	37
1	2		5				9			11	10	4					8				7	6	10*	3	12	38
34	36	18	32	29	28	20	29	31	7	37	19	11	4	13	1	4	22	4	1	15	6	15	2			
		2					6	2			4	7	6	12	1	4	3	1	1	2		1	1	3	1	
		1	5	1	4	5	10			9	2		3				4									

59

1997-98

1	Aug	9	(h)	Crystal Palace	L	1-2	Ferguson	35,716
2		23	(h)	West Ham U	W	2-1	Speed, Stuart	34,356
3		27	(h)	Manchester U	L	0-2		40,479
4	Sep	1	(a)	Bolton W	D	0-0		23,131
5		13	(a)	Derby Co	L	1-3	Stuart	27,828
6		20	(h)	Barnsley	W	4-2	Speed 2 (1 pen), Cadamarteri, Oster	32,659
7		24	(a)	Newcastle U	L	0-1		36,705
8		27	(h)	Arsenal	D	2-2	Ball, Cadamarteri	35,457
9	Oct	4	(a)	Sheffield W	L	1-3	Cadamarteri	24,483
10		18	(h)	Liverpool	W	2-0	Ruddock (og), Cadamarteri	40,112
11		25	(a)	Coventry C	D	0-0		18,755
12	Nov	2	(h)	Southampton	L	0-2		29,565
13		8	(a)	Blackburn R	L	2-3	Speed, Ferguson	25,397
14		22	(a)	Aston Villa	L	1-2	Speed (pen)	36,389
15		26	(a)	Chelsea	L	0-2		32,736
16		29	(h)	Tottenham H	L	0-2		36,670
17	Dec	6	(a)	Leeds U	D	0-0		34,872
18		13	(h)	Wimbledon	D	0-0		28,533
19		20	(a)	Leicester C	W	1-0	Speed (pen)	20,628
20		26	(a)	Manchester U	L	0-2		55,167
21		28	(h)	Bolton W	W	3-2	Ferguson 3	37,149
22	Jan	10	(a)	Crystal Palace	W	3-1	Barmby, Ferguson, Madar	23,311
23		18	(h)	Chelsea	W	3-1	Speed, Ferguson, Duberry (og)	32,355
24		31	(a)	West Ham U	D	2-2	Barmby, Madar	25,905
25	Feb	7	(a)	Barnsley	D	2-2	Ferguson, Grant	18,654
26		14	(h)	Derby Co	L	1-2	Thomsen	34,876
27		23	(a)	Liverpool	D	1-1	Ferguson	44,501
28		28	(h)	Newcastle U	D	0-0		37,972
29	Mar	7	(a)	Southampton	L	1-2	Tiler	15,102
30		14	(h)	Blackburn R	W	1-0	Madar	33,423
31		28	(h)	Aston Villa	L	1-4	Madar	36,471
32	Apr	4	(a)	Tottenham H	D	1-1	Madar	35,624
33		11	(h)	Leeds U	W	2-0	Hutchison, Ferguson	37,099
34		13	(a)	Wimbledon	D	0-0		15,131
35		18	(h)	Leicester C	D	1-1	Madar	33,642
36		25	(h)	Sheffield W	L	1-3	Ferguson	35,497
37	May	3	(a)	Arsenal	L	0-4		38,269
38		10	(h)	Coventry C	D	1-1	Farrelly	40,109

FINAL LEAGUE POSITION: 17th in F.A. Carling Premiership

Appearances

Sub. Appearances

Goals

Southall	Thomas	Phelan	Thomsen	Watson	Bilic	Stuart	Farrelly	Ferguson	Oster	Speed	Branch	Barmby	Short	Williamson	Barrett	Hinchcliffe	Cadamarteri	Gerrard	Grant	McCann	Ball	O'Connor	Ward	Tiler	Myhre	Allen	Jeffers	Dunne	Madar	O'Kane	Hutchison	Spencer	Beagrie	
1	2*	3	4†	5	6	7	8	9	10°	11	12	13	14																					1
1		3		5	6	7	10†	9	13	11		8	12	4*	2																			2
1	12	3		5	6	7		9	13	11	14	8†	4°	10	2*																			3
1	2°	3		5*	6	7		9	10	11	13	8†	12	4			14																	4
1					6	7		9	10	11	8†	12	5	4	2*	3	13																	5
				5	6	7	12	9	13	11		8°	2	4*		3	10†	1																6
				5	6	7	12		10	11		8°			2	3	9*	1	4†	13	14													7
		3		5	6	7			10	11				2			9	1	8*	12	4													8
	2†			5	6	7			10	11	12	13		4		3	9	1	8*															9
1				5		7		9	10*	11			6	4	2	3	8†			12	13													10
1				5		7		9	10	11	12		6	4	2	3	8*																	11
1	12			5		7		9	10	11	13		6	4	2*	3	8†																	12
1	3			6	7°	12	9	13	10	14			5	4*	2	11	8†																	13
1	3			6	7	12	9	13	11		8		5	4*	2°	3	10†						14											14
1	3°			6		10†	9	12	11	8			4	7	5*	13				14			2											15
1	3†			6		10*	9	12	11	8			4°	7	13	14							2	5										16
				5		7	9		11	8			4	10		3							2	6	1									17
				5		7		12	11	8			4	10*	13	3	9						2†	6	1									18
				5		7	10*		11	8			4	2	3		9				12			6	1									19
			12	5°		7	10			8			4	2†	3	9				11*				6	1	13	14							20
	2	12				7	9	10*		8				3	11					4			6	1				5						21
	2	14		6		12	9		11	8			4	13†					10*		3			5	1				7†					22
		12		6		13	9		11	8	4*								10	3			5	1	2				7†					23
				5	6	7	9				8						12		10	4			2	1	13			11*	3†					24
		12		5		7	9	13			8*	4					14		10	3			2	1				11°	6†					25
	2	12		5	13	7	9	10				4†					14	8*	3			6	1				11°							26
			8	5	6	7	9	12								10*	13	3		2	4	1						11†						27
				5		7		12			4					9			3	2†	6	1	13				11	8*	10					28
				5	6	7*	10				8					12			3	4	1					9	2	11						29
				5	6		10			8†						12	13	3		4	1					9*	2	11	7					30
				5	7*	10°	8	4†						12			2			1				13	9	3	6	11	14					31
				5		9	8	4						10	3				1				6	7*	2	11	12							32
			12	9†			8*	4						7	3				5	1				13	2	6	10	11						33
			12	9	13		8†	4						6	3				5	1				10*	2	7	14	11°						34
			12	7	9	13		4						6*	3				5	1				10†	2	8	14	11°						35
			12	6		9	13	8	4†					7	3				5*	1		2°			10		11		14					36
			5	6*		12	9	13			8	4					3		7	1				14	2†	10		11°						37
			5	/†	9		8	4									12		13	3			6	1		11*	2	10						38
12	6	8	2	25	2	14	18	28	16	21	1	26	27	15	12	15	15	4	7	5	21	8	19		22	2		2	15	12	11	3	4	
	1	1	6	1	2		8	1	15	5	4	4	1	2	11		6		4	1						3	1	1	2			3	2	
	1			2		1	11	1	7		2						4		1	1			1			1			6		1			

1998-99

1	Aug	15	(h)	Aston Villa	D	0-0		40,112
2		22	(a)	Leicester C	L	0-2		21,037
3		29	(h)	Tottenham H	L	0-1		39,378
4	Sep	8	(a)	Nottingham F	W	2-0	Ferguson 2	25,610
5		12	(h)	Leeds U	D	0-0		36,687
6		19	(a)	Middlesbrough	D	2-2	Ball (pen), Collins	34,563
7		26	(h)	Blackburn R	D	0-0		36,404
8	Oct	3	(a)	Wimbledon	W	2-1	Cadamarteri, Ferguson	16,054
9		17	(h)	Liverpool	D	0-0		40,185
10		24	(a)	Sheffield W	D	0-0		26,592
11		31	(h)	Manchester U	L	1-4	Ferguson	40,087
12	Nov	8	(a)	Arsenal	L	0-1		38,088
13		15	(a)	Coventry C	L	0-3		19,279
14		23	(h)	Newcastle U	W	1-0	Ball (pen)	30,357
15		28	(a)	Charlton Ath	W	2-1	Cadamarteri 2	20,043
16	Dec	5	(h)	Chelsea	D	0-0		36,430
17		12	(h)	Southampton	W	1-0	Bakayoko	32,073
18		19	(a)	West Ham U	L	1-2	Cadamarteri	25,998
19		26	(h)	Derby Co	D	0-0		39,206
20		28	(a)	Tottenham H	L	1-4	Bakayoko	36,053
21	Jan	9	(h)	Leicester C	D	0-0		32,792
22		18	(a)	Aston Villa	L	0-3		32,488
23		30	(h)	Nottingham F	L	0-1		34,175
24	Feb	7	(a)	Derby Co	L	1-2	Barmby	27,603
25		17	(h)	Middlesbrough	W	5-0	Barmby 2, Dacourt, Materazzi, Unsworth	31,606
26		20	(a)	Leeds U	L	0-1		36,344
27		27	(h)	Wimbledon	D	1-1	Jeffers	32,574
28	Mar	10	(a)	Blackburn R	W	2-1	Bakayoko 2	27,219
29		13	(h)	Arsenal	L	0-2		38,049
30		21	(a)	Manchester U	L	1-3	Hutchison	55,182
31	Apr	3	(a)	Liverpool	L	2-3	Dacourt, Jeffers	44,852
32		5	(h)	Sheffield W	L	1-2	Jeffers	35,270
33		11	(h)	Coventry C	W	2-0	Campbell 2	32,341
34		17	(a)	Newcastle U	W	3-1	Campbell 2, Gemmill	36,775
35		24	(h)	Charlton Ath	W	4-1	Hutchison, Campbell 2, Jeffers	40,089
36	May	1	(a)	Chelsea	L	1-3	Jeffers	34,000
37		8	(h)	West Ham U	W	6-0	Campbell 3, Ball (pen), Hutchison, Jeffers	40,029
38		16	(a)	Southampton	L	0-2		15,254

FINAL LEAGUE POSITION: 14th in F.A. Carling Premiership

Appearances

Sub. Appearances

Goals

Myhre	Cleland	Ball	Short	Materazzi	Tiler	Collins	Barmby	Ferguson	Dacourt	Spencer	Hutchison	Cadamarteri	Unsworth	Watson	Thomas	Farrelly	Oster	Grant	Bakayoko	Ward	Dunne	Milligan	Jeffers	Bilic	Madar	Branch	Farley	Weir	Jevons	O'Kane	Degn	Gemmill	Campbell	No.
1	2	3	4	5	6	7	8	9	10*	11†	12	13																						1
1	2	3	4	5°	6	7	8†	9	10	11*	13	12	14																					2
1	2*	3	4	5		7	8†	9	10	13	12	11	6																					3
1	2	3		6		7	8*	9†	10		11	12	4	5	13																			4
1	2	3		6		7	8*	9	10		11†	12	4	5		13																		5
1	2	3		6		7	8	9	10		11*	12	4	5																				6
1	2†	3	10	6		7	8*	9			11	12	4	5			13																	7
1		3	2	6		7		9	10		11	8	4	5																				8
1	2	3	4			7		9			11	12	6	5			8*	10†	13															9
1	2	3		6		7		9	10		8	12	4	5					11*															10
1		3	2*	6		7		9	10			8	4	5					11			12												11
1	2*	3		6°		7		9	10	12	13	8		5†					11	4		14												12
1	2†	3	4	5		7		9		10	12		6					8	11*				13											13
1		3	4			7				10	9†		6	5				8	11*	2	12	13												14
1	12	3	4	13		7				10	9		6	5†			14	8°	11*		2													15
1	2	3	4	5		7				10	9		6					8	11															16
1	2	3				7	12		13	10			6					8*	11	4				5	9†									17
1	3			5		12	13		10		11	7	6					8†	2*					4	9°	14								18
1		3		6		7†	12		10		11	8*	4						9	2				5	13									19
1	12	3	4*			7°	8		10		11	13	6				14		9†	2			5											20
1	2	3					12		10		11	7*	6	5			8		9	4														21
1	2	3		6			8		10		11	12		5			4*	7†	9°			13												22
1		3		5			8		12		11	9†	6				10	7*	13	2°		4												23
1		3					8		10			6		5			4*		9	7	2		11		12									24
1		3		5			8		10		11		6				4†	7	12	2		9*		13										25
1		3		5			8		10		11	12	6				4°	7†	13	2		9*		14										26
1	11	3		6			8	9	10			3	5				4*		7		12		2											27
1	3		4	5			8°		10			6						12	9*	2			13		7	14		11†						28
1	3			6			8*		10		11	12	4	5				13	9°	2†		14			7									29
1	3		4	5					10		11	12	6					8°	9*				13			2			7†	14				30
1		3	2	6°			8†		10			12	4	5					13				11*		14							7	9	31
1	12	3	4	5*			8†		10				6°					13					11			2			14			7	9	32
1		3	4	6			8		10			5						12					11*			2						7	9	33
1		3	4						10	11	12		6	5				13					8*			2						7	9†	34
1		3	4						10	11			6	5									8			2						7	9	35
1		3	4				8			11	12		6					7*	5†				10			2				13			9	36
1		3	4						10	11			6	5									8			2						7	9	37
1		3	4*						10	11	12		6	5				13					8†			2			14			7°	9	38
38	16	36	22	26	2	19	20	13	28	2	29	11	33	22			6	13	17	4	15		11	4	2	1		11		2		7	8	
	2	1		1		1	4		2	1	4	19	1		1	1	3	3	6	2	1	3	4		6	1	3	1		4				
		3	1	1		1	3	4	2		3	4	1					4	6													1	9	

F.A. CUP COMPETITION

1974/75 SEASON
3rd Round
Jan 4 vs Altrincham (h) 1-1
Att: 34,519   Clements (pen)
Replay (at Old Trafford)
Jan 7 vs Altrincham (a) 2-0
Att: 35,530   Latchford, Lyons
4th Round
Jan 25 vs Plymouth Argyle (a) 3-1
Att: 38,000   Pearson, Lyons 2
5th Round
Feb 15 vs Fulham (h) 1-2
Att: 45,223   Kenyon

1975/76 SEASON
3rd Round
Jan 3 vs Derby County (a) 1-2
Att: 31,647   Jones

1976/77 SEASON
3rd Round
Jan 8 vs Stoke City (h) 2-0
Att: 32,952   Lyons, McKenzie (pen)
4th Round
Jan 29 vs Swindon Town (a) 2-2
Att: 24,347   McKenzie, Latchford
Replay
Feb 1 vs Swindon Town (h) 2-1
Att: 38,063   Dobson, Jones
5th Round
Feb 26 vs Cardiff City (a) 2-1
Att: 35,582   Latchford, McKenzie
6th Round
Mar 19 vs Derby County (h) 2-0
Att: 42,409   Latchford, Pearson
Semi-Final (at Maine Road)
Apr 23 vs Liverpool 2-2
Att: 52,637   McKenzie, Rioch
Replay (at Maine Road)
Apr 27 vs Liverpool 0-3
Att: 52,579

1977/78 SEASON
3rd Round
Jan 7 vs Aston Villa (h) 4-1
Att: 46,320   King, Ross (pen), McKenzie, Latchford
4th Round
Jan 28 vs Middlesbrough (a) 2-3
Att: 33,692   Telfer, Lyons

1978/79 SEASON
3rd Round
Jan 10 vs Sunderland (a) 1-2
Att: 28,602   Dobson

1979/80 SEASON
3rd Round
Jan 5 vs Aldershot (h) 4-1
Att: 23,700   Latchford, Hartford, King, Kidd
4th Round
Jan 26 vs Wigan Athletic (h) 3-0
Att: 51,853   McBride, Latchford, Kidd
5th Round
Feb 16 vs Wrexham (h) 5-2
Att: 44,830   Megson, Eastoe 2, Ross (pen), Latchford
6th Round
Mar 8 vs Ipswich Town (h) 2-1
Att: 45,104   Latchford, Kidd
Semi-Final (at Villa Park)
Apr 12 vs West Ham United 1-1
Att: 47,685   Kidd (pen)

Replay (at Elland Road)
Apr 16 vs West Ham United 1-2
Att: 40,720   Latchford

1980/81 SEASON
3rd Round
Jan 3 vs Arsenal (h) 2-0
Att: 34,240   Sansom (og), Lyons
4th Round
Jan 24 vs Liverpool (h) 2-1
Att: 53,084   Cohen (og), Varadi
5th Round
Feb 14 vs Southampton (a) 0-0
Att: 24,152
Replay
Feb 17 vs Southampton (h) 1-0 (aet.)
Att: 49,192   O'Keefe
6th Round
Mar 7 vs Manchester City (h) 2-2
Att: 52,791   Eastoe, Ross (pen)
Replay
Mar 11 vs Manchester City (a) 1-3
Att: 52,532   Eastoe

1981/82 SEASON
3rd Round
Jan 2 vs West Ham United (a) 1-2
Att: 24,431   Eastoe

1982/83 SEASON
3rd Round
Jan 8 vs Newport County (a) 1-1
Att: 9,527   Sheedy
Replay
Jan 11 vs Newport County (h) 2-1
Att: 18,565   Sharp, King
4th Round
Jan 30 vs Shrewsbury Town (h) 2-1
Att: 35,188   Sheedy, Heath
5th Round
Feb 19 vs Tottenham Hotspur (h) 2-0
Att: 42,995   King, Sharp
6th Round
Mar 12 vs Manchester United (a) 0-1
Att: 58,198

1983/84 SEASON
3rd Round
Jan 6 vs Stoke City (a) 2-0
Att: 16,462   Gray, Irvine
4th Round
Jan 28 vs Gillingham (h) 0-0
Att: 22,380
Replay
Jan 31 vs Gillingham (a) 0-0 (aet.)
Att: 15,339
2nd Replay
Feb 6 vs Gillingham (a) 3-0
Att: 17,817   Sheedy 2, Heath
5th Round
Feb 18 vs Shrewsbury Town (h) 3-0
Att: 27,106   Irvine, Reid, Griffin (og)
6th Round
Mar 10 vs Notts County (a) 2-1
Att: 19,534   Richardson, Gray
Semi-Final (at Highbury)
Apr 14 vs Southampton 1-0 (aet.)
Att: 46,587   Heath
FINAL (at Wembley)
May 19 vs Watford 2-0
Att: 100,000   Sharp, Gray

1984/85 SEASON
3rd Round
Jan 5 vs Leeds United (a) 2-0
Att: 21,211   Sharp (pen), Sheedy

4th Round
Jan 26 vs Doncaster Rovers (h) 2-0
Att: 37,537   Steven, Stevens
5th Round
Feb 16 vs Telford United (h) 3-0
Att: 47,402   Reid, Sheedy (pen), Steven
6th Round
Mar 9 vs Ipswich Town (h) 2-2
Att: 36,468   Sheedy, Mountfield
Replay
Mar 13 vs Ipswich Town (a) 1-0
Att: 27,737   Sharp (pen)
Semi-Final (at Villa Park)
Apr 13 vs Luton T. 2-1 (aet.) (90 mins 1-1)
Att: 45,289   Sheedy, Mountfield
FINAL (at Wembley)
May 18 vs Manchester United 0-1
Att: 100,000

1985/86 SEASON
3rd Round
Jan 5 vs Exeter City (h) 1-0
Att: 22,726   Stevens
4th Round
Jan 25 vs Blackburn Rovers (h) 3-1
Att: 41,831   Van den Hauwe, Lineker 2
5th Round
Mar 4 vs Tottenham Hotspur (a) 2-1
Att: 23,338   Heath, Lineker
6th Round
Mar 8 vs Luton Town (a) 2-2
Att: 15,529   Donaghy (og), Heath
Replay
Mar 12 vs Luton Town (h) 1-0
Att: 44,264   Lineker
Semi-Final (at Villa Park)
Apr 5 vs Sheffield Wednesday 2-1
Att: 47,711   Harper, Sharp
FINAL (at Wembley)
May 10 vs Liverpool 1-3
Att: 98,000   Lineker

1986/87 SEASON
3rd Round
Jan 10 vs Southampton (h) 2-1
Att: 32,320   Sharp 2
4th Round
Jan 31 vs Bradford City (h) 1-0
Att: 15,519   Snodin
5th Round
Feb 22 vs Wimbledon (a) 1-3
Att: 9,924   Wilkinson

1987/88 SEASON
3rd Round
Jan 9 vs Sheffield Wednesday (a) 1-1
Att: 33,304   Reid
Replay
Jan 13 vs Sheffield Wednesday (h) 1-1 (aet.)
Att: 32,935   Chapman
2nd Replay
Jan 25 vs Sheffield Wednesday (h) 1-1 (aet.)
Att: 37,414   Chapman
3rd Replay
Jan 27 vs Sheffield Wednesday (h) 5-0
Att: 38,953   Sharp 3, Heath, Snodin
4th Round
Jan 30 vs Middlesbrough (h) 1-1
Att: 36,564   Sharp
Replay
Feb 3 vs Middlesbrough (a) 2-2 (aet.)
Att: 25,235   Watson, Steven
2nd Replay
Feb 9 vs Middlesbrough (h) 2-1
Att: 32,222   Sharp, Mowbray (og)

5th Round
Feb 21 vs Liverpool (h) 0-1
Att: 48,270

1988/89 SEASON
3rd Round
Jan 7 vs West Bromwich Albion (a) 1-1
Att: 31,186 Sheedy (pen)
Replay
Jan 11 vs West Bromwich Albion (h) 1-0
Att: 31,697 Sheedy
4th Round
Jan 28 vs Plymouth Argyle (a) 1-1
Att: 27,566 Sheedy (pen)
Replay
Jan 31 vs Plymouth Argyle (h) 4-0
Att: 28,542 Sharp 2, Nevin, Sheedy
5th Round
Feb 18 vs Barnsley (a) 1-0
Att: 32,551 Sharp
6th Round
Mar 19 vs Wimbledon (h) 1-0
Att: 24,562 McCall
Semi-Final (at Villa Park)
Apr 15 vs Norwich City 1-0
Att: 46,533 Nevin
FINAL (at Wembley)
May 20 vs Liverpool 2-3
Att: 82,800 McCall 2

1989/90 SEASON
3rd Round
Jan 6 vs Middlesbrough (a) 0-0
Att: 20,075
Replay
Jan 10 vs Middlesbrough (h) 1-1 (aet.)
Att: 24,352 Sheedy
2nd Replay
Jan 17 vs Middlesbrough (a) 1-0
Att: 23,866 Whiteside
4th Round
Jan 28 vs Sheffield Wednesday (a) 2-1
Att: 31,754 Whiteside 2
5th Round
Feb 17 vs Oldham Athletic (a) 2-2
Att: 19,320 Sharp, Cottee
Replay
Feb 21 vs Oldham Athletic (h) 1-1 (aet.)
Att: 36,663 Sheedy (pen)
2nd Replay
Mar 10 vs Oldham Athletic (a) 1-2 (aet.)
Att: 19,346 Cottee

1990/91 SEASON
3rd Round
Jan 5 vs Charlton Athletic (a) 2-1
Att: 12,234 Ebbrell 2
4th Round
Jan 27 vs Woking (h) 1-0
Att: 34,724 Sheedy
5th Round
Feb 17 vs Liverpool (a) 0-0
Att: 38,323
Replay
Feb 20 vs Liverpool (h) 4-4 (aet.)
Att: 37,766 Cottee 2, Sharp 2
2nd Replay
Feb 27 vs Liverpool (h) 1-0
Att: 40,201 Watson
6th Round
Mar 11 vs West Ham United (a) 1-2
Att: 28,162 Watson

1991/92 SEASON
3rd Round
Jan 4 vs Southend United (h) 1-0
Att: 22,606 Beardsley

4th Round
Jan 26 vs Chelsea (a) 0-1
Att: 21,152

1992/93 SEASON
3rd Round
Jan 2 vs Wimbledon (h) 0-0
Att: 7,818
Replay
Jan 12 vs Wimbledon (a) 1-2
Att: 15,293 Watson

1993/94 SEASON
3rd Round
Jan 8 vs Bolton Wanderers (a) 1-1
Att: 21,702 Rideout
Replay
Jan 19 vs Bolton Wanderers (h) 2-3 (aet.)
Att: 34,642 Barlow 2

1994/95 SEASON
3rd Round
Jan 7 vs Derby County (h) 1-0
Att: 29,406 Hinchcliffe
4th Round
Jan 29 vs Bristol City (a) 1-0
Att: 19,816 Jackson
5th Round
Feb 18 vs Norwich City (h) 5-0
Att: 31,616 Limpar, Parkinson, Rideout, Ferguson, Stuart
6th Round
Mar 12 vs Newcastle United (h) 1-0
Att: 35,203 Watson
Semi-Final (at Elland Road)
Apr 9 vs Tottenham Hotspur 4-1
Att: 38,226 Jackson, Stuart, Amokachi 2
FINAL (at Wembley)
May 20 vs Manchester United 1-0
Att: 79,592 Rideout

1995/96 SEASON
3rd Round
Jan 7 vs Stockport County (h) 2-1
Att: 28,921 Ablett, Stuart
4th Round
Jan 27 vs Port Vale (h) 2-2
Att: 33,168 Amokachi, Ferguson
Replay
Feb 14 vs Port Vale (a) 1-2
Att: 19,197 Stuart

1996/97 SEASON
3rd Round
Jan 5 vs Swindon Town (h) 3-0
Att: 20,411 Kanchelskis (pen), Barmby, Ferguson
4th Round
Jan 25 vs Bradford City (h) 2-3
Att: 30,007 O'Brien (og), Speed

1997/98 SEASON
3rd Round
Jan 4 vs Newcastle United (h) 0-1
Att: 20,885

1998/99 SEASON
3rd Round
Jan 2 vs Bristol City (a) 2-0
Att: 19,608 Bakayoko 2
4th Round
Jan 23 vs Ipswich Town (h) 1-0
Att: 28,854 Barmby
5th Round
Feb 13 vs Coventry City (h) 2-1
Att: 33,907 Jeffers, Oster
6th Round
Mar 7 vs Newcastle United (h) 1-4
Att: 36,504 Unsworth

LEAGUE CUP COMPETITION

1975/76 SEASON
2nd Round
Sep 9 vs Arsenal (h) 2-2
Att: 17,174 Smallman, Lyons
Replay
Sep 23 vs Arsenal (a) 1-0
Att: 21,813 Kenyon
3rd Round
Oct 8 vs Carlisle United (h) 2-0
Att: 20,010 Latchford, Dobson
4th Round
Nov 11 vs Notts County (h) 2-2
Att: 19,169 Jones, Irving
Replay
Nov 25 vs Notts County (a) 0-2
Att: 23,323

1976/77 SEASON
2nd Round
Aug 30 vs Cambridge United (h) 3-0
Att: 10,898 Latchford, Dobson, King
3rd Round
Sep 20 vs Stockport County (a) 1-0
Att: 15,700 Latchford
4th Round
Oct 26 vs Coventry City (h) 3-0
Att: 21,572 King 2, Lyons
5th Round
Dec 1 vs Manchester United (a) 3-0
Att: 57,738 King 2, Dobson
Semi-Final (1st leg)
Jan 18 vs Bolton Wanderers (h) 1-1
Att: 48,000 McKenzie
Semi-Final (2nd leg)
Feb 15 vs Bolton Wands. (a) 1-0 (agg. 2-1)
Att: 50,413 Latchford
FINAL (at Wembley)
Mar 12 vs Aston Villa 0-0
Att: 100,000
Replay (at Hillsborough)
Mar 16 vs Aston Villa 1-1
Att: 55,000 Latchford
2nd Replay (at Old Trafford)
Apr 13 vs Aston Villa 2-3 (aet.)
Att: 54,749 Latchford, Lyons

1977/78 SEASON
2nd Round
Aug 30 vs Sheffield United (a) 3-0
Att: 18,571 Latchford, McKenzie, King
3rd Round
Oct 25 vs Middlesbrough (a) 2-2
Att: 32,766 King, Telfer
Replay
Oct 31 vs Middlesbrough (h) 2-1
Att: 28,500 Lyons, Pearson
4th Round
Nov 29 vs Sheffield Wednesday (a) 3-1
Att: 36,079 Lyons, Dobson, Pearson
5th Round
Jan 18 vs Leeds United (a) 1-4
Att: 35,020 Thomas

1978/79 SEASON
2nd Round
Aug 29 vs Wimbledon (h) 8-0
Att: 23,137 Latchford 5 (1 pen), Dobson 3
3rd Round
Oct 3 vs Darlington (h) 1-0
Att: 23,682 Dobson
4th Round
Nov 7 vs Nottingham Forest (h) 2-3
Att: 48,503 Burns (og), Latchford

1979/80 SEASON
2nd Round (1st leg)
Aug 28 vs Cardiff City (h) 2-0
Att: 18,061   Kidd 2
2nd Round (2nd leg)
Sep 5 vs Cardiff City (a) 0-1 (agg. 2-1)
Att: 9,698
3rd Round
Sep 25 vs Aston Villa (a) 0-0
Att: 22,635
Replay
Oct 9 vs Aston Villa (h) 4-1
Att: 22,080   Kidd, Latchford 2, Rimmer (og)
4th Round
Oct 30 vs Grimsby Town (a) 1-2
Att: 22,043   Kidd

1980/81 SEASON
2nd Round (1st leg)
Aug 26 vs Blackpool (h) 3-0
Att: 20,156   Eastoe, Latchford, McBride
2nd Round (2nd leg)
Sep 3 vs Blackpool (a) 2-2 (aggregate 5-2)
Att: 10,579   Latchford 2
3rd Round
Sep 24 vs West Bromwich Albion (h) 1-2
Att: 23,436   Gidman

1981/82 SEASON
2nd Round (1st leg)
Oct 6 vs Coventry City (h) 1-1
Att: 17,228   Ferguson
2nd Round (2nd leg)
Oct 27 vs Coventry City (a) 1-0 (agg. 2-1)
Att: 13,770   Ferguson
3rd Round
Nov 11 vs Oxford United (h) 1-0
Att: 14,910   O'Keefe
4th Round
Dec 15 vs Ipswich Town (h) 2-3
Att: 15,759   McMahon 2

1982/83 SEASON
2nd Round (1st leg)
Oct 5 vs Newport County (a) 2-0
Att: 8,293   McMahon, King
2nd Round (2nd leg)
Oct 27 vs Newport County (h) 2-2 (agg. 4-2)
Att: 8,941   King, Johnson
3rd Round
Nov 9 vs Arsenal (h) 1-1
Att: 13,089   Stevens
Replay
Nov 23 vs Arsenal (a) 0-3
Att: 19,547

1983/84 SEASON
2nd Round (1st leg)
Oct 4 vs Chesterfield (a) 1-0
Att: 10,713   Sharp
2nd Round (2nd leg)
Oct 26 vs Chesterfield (h) 2-2 (agg. 3-2)
Att: 8,067   Heath, Steven
3rd Round
Nov 9 vs Coventry City (h) 2-1
Att: 9,080   Heath, Sharp
4th Round
Nov 30 vs West Ham United (a) 2-2
Att: 19,702   Reid, Sheedy
Replay
Dec 6 vs West Ham United (h) 2-0 (aet.)
Att: 21,609   King, Sheedy
5th Round
Jan 18 vs Oxford United (h) 1-1
Att: 14,333   Heath

Replay
Jan 24 vs Oxford United (h) 4-1
Att: 31,011   Richardson, Sheedy, Heath, Sharp
Semi-Final (1st leg)
Feb 15 vs Aston Villa (h) 2-0
Att: 40,006   Sheedy, Richardson
Semi-Final (2nd leg)
Feb 22 vs Aston Villa (a) 0-1 (agg. 2-1)
Att: 42,426
FINAL (at Wembley)
Mar 25 vs Liverpool 0-0 (aet.)
Att: 100,000
Replay (at Maine Road)
Mar 28 vs Liverpool 0-1
Att: 52,089

1984/85 SEASON
2nd Round (1st leg)
Sep 26 vs Sheffield United (a) 2-2
Att: 16,345   Sharp, Mountfield
2nd Round (2nd leg)
Oct 10 vs Sheffield United (h) 4-0 (agg. 6-2)
Att: 18,740   Mountfield, Bracewell, Sharp, Heath
3rd Round
Oct 30 vs Manchester United (a) 2-1
Att: 50,918   Sharp (pen), Gidman (og)
4th Round
Nov 20 vs Grimsby Town (h) 0-1
Att: 26,298

1985/86 SEASON
2nd Round (1st leg)
Sep 25 vs Bournemouth (h) 3-2
Att: 13,930   Lineker, Marshall, Hefferman
2nd Round (2nd leg)
Oct 8 vs Bournemouth (a) 2-0 (agg. 5-2)
Att: 8,081   Lineker, Richardson
3rd Round
Oct 29 vs Shrewsbury Town (a) 4-1
Att: 10,246   Sharp, Hughes (og), Sheedy, Heath
4th Round
Nov 26 vs Chelsea (a) 2-2
Att: 27,544   Sheedy, Bracewell
Replay
Dec 10 vs Chelsea (h) 1-2
Att: 26,376   Lineker

1986/87 SEASON
2nd Round (1st leg)
Sep 24 vs Newport County (h) 4-0
Att: 11,957   Langley, Heath, Wilkinson 2
2nd Round (2nd leg)
Oct 7 vs Newport County (a) 5-1 (agg. 9-1)
Att: 7,172   Wilkinson 3, Sharp, Mullen (og)
3rd Round
Oct 28 vs Sheffield Wednesday (h) 4-0
Att: 24,638   Wilkinson 2, Heath, Mountfield
4th Round
Nov 19 vs Norwich City (a) 4-1
Att: 17,988   Sheedy, Sharp, Steven (pen), Heath
5th Round
Jan 21 vs Liverpool (h) 0-1
Att: 53,323

1987/88 SEASON
2nd Round (1st leg)
Sep 22 vs Rotherham United (h) 3-2
Att: 15,369   Snodin, Wilson, Clarke (pen)
2nd Round (2nd leg)
Oct 6 vs Rotherham Utd. (a) 0-0 (agg. 3-2)
Att: 12,995
3rd Round
Oct 28 vs Liverpool (a) 1-0
Att: 44,071   Stevens

4th Round
Nov 17 vs Oldham Athletic (h) 2-1
Att: 23,315   Watson, Adams
5th Round
Jan 20 vs Manchester City (h) 2-0
Att: 40,014   Heath, Sharp
Semi-Final (1st leg)
Feb 7 vs Arsenal (h) 0-1
Att: 25,476
Semi-Final (2nd leg)
Feb 24 vs Arsenal (a) 1-3 (aggregate 1-4)
Att: 51,148   Heath

1988/89 SEASON
2nd Round (1st leg)
Sep 27 vs Bury (h) 3-0
Att: 11,071   Sharp, McDonald (pen), McCall
2nd Round (2nd leg)
Oct 11 vs Bury (a) 2-2 (aggregate 5-2)
Att: 4,592   Steven (pen), Sharp
3rd Round
Nov 8 vs Oldham Athletic (h) 1-1
Att: 17,230   Steven (pen)
Replay
Nov 29 vs Oldham Athletic (a) 2-0
Att: 14,573   Cottee 2
4th Round
Dec 14 vs Bradford City (a) 1-3
Att: 15,055   Watson

1989/90 SEASON
2nd Round (1st leg)
Sep 19 vs Leyton Orient (a) 2-0
Att: 8,214   Newell, Sheedy
2nd Round (2nd leg)
Oct 3 vs Leyton Orient (h) 2-2 (agg. 4-2)
Att: 10,128   Whiteside, Sheedy
3rd Round
Oct 24 vs Luton Town (h) 3-0
Att: 18,428   Newell 2, Nevin
4th Round
Nov 22 vs Nottingham Forest (a) 0-1
Att: 21,324

1990/91 SEASON
2nd Round (1st leg)
Sep 25 vs Wrexham (a) 5-0
Att: 9,072   Cottee 3, McDonald, Nevin
2nd Round (2nd leg)
Oct 9 vs Wrexham (h) 6-0 (aggregate 11-0)
Att: 7,415   Sharp 3, Cottee, Ebbrell, McDonald
3rd Round
Oct 30 vs Sheffield United (a) 1-2
Att: 15,045   Pemberton (og)

1991/92 SEASON
2nd Round (1st leg)
Sep 24 vs Watford (h) 1-0
Att: 8,264   Beardsley
2nd Round (2nd leg)
Oct 8 vs Watford (a) 2-1 (aggregate 3-1)
Att: 11,561   Newell, Beardsley
3rd Round
Oct 30 vs Wolverhampton Wands. (h) 4-1
Att: 19,065   Beagrie 2, Cottee, Beardsley
4th Round
Dec 4 vs Leeds United (h) 1-4
Att: 25,467   Atteveld

1992/93 SEASON
2nd Round (1st leg)
Sep 23 vs Rotherham United (a) 0-1
Att: 7,736
2nd Round (2nd leg)
Oct 7 vs Rotherham Utd. (h) 3-0 (agg. 3-1)
Att: 10,302   Rideout 2, Cottee

3rd Round
Oct 28 vs Wimbledon (h) 0-0
Att: 9,541
Replay
Nov 10 vs Wimbledon (a) 1-0
Att: 3,686   Beardsley
4th Round
Dec 2 vs Chelsea (h) 2-2
Att: 14,457   Barlow, Beardsley
Replay
Dec 16 vs Chelsea (a) 0-1
Att: 19,496

1993/94 SEASON
2nd Round (1st leg)
Sep 21 vs Lincoln City (a) 4-3
Att: 9,153   Rideout 3, Cottee
2nd Round (2nd leg)
Oct 6 vs Lincoln City (h) 4-2 (agg. 8-5)
Att: 8,375   Rideout, Snodin, Cottee 2
3rd Round
Oct 26 vs Crystal Palace (h) 2-2
Att: 11,547   Beagrie, Watson
Replay
Nov 10 vs Crystal Palace (a) 4-1
*Att: 14,662   Watson 2, Ward (pen),
Young (og)*
4th Round
Nov 30 vs Manchester United (h) 0-2
Att: 34,052

1994/95 SEASON
2nd Round (1st leg)
Sep 20 vs Portsmouth (h) 2-3
Att: 14,043   Samways, Stuart (pen)
2nd Round (2nd leg)
Oct 5 vs Portsmouth (a) 1-1 (aggregate 3-4)
Att: 13,605   Watson

1995/96 SEASON
2nd Round (1st leg)
Sep 20 vs Millwall (a) 0-0
Att: 12,053
2nd Round (2nd leg)
Oct 4 vs Millwall (h) 2-4 (aggregate 2-4)
Att: 14,891   Hinchcliffe (pen), Stuart

1996/97 SEASON
2nd Round (1st leg)
Sep 18 vs York City (h) 1-1
Att: 11,527   Kanchelskis
2nd Round (2nd leg)
Sep 24 vs York City (a) 2-3 (aggregate 3-4)
Att: 7,854   Rideout, Speed

1997/98 SEASON
2nd Round (1st leg)
Sep 16 vs Scunthorpe United (a) 1-0
Att: 7,145   Farrelly
2nd Round (2nd leg)
Oct 1 vs Scunthorpe Utd. (h) 5-0 (agg. 6-0)
*Att: 11,562   Stuart, Oster 2, Barmby,
Cadamarteri*
3rd Round
Oct 15 vs Coventry City (a) 1-4
Att: 10,087   Barmby

1998/99 SEASON
2nd Round (1st leg)
Sep 15 vs Huddersfield Town (a) 1-1
Att: 15,395   Watson
2nd Round (2nd leg)
Sep 23 vs Huddersfield T. (h) 2-1 (agg. 3-2)
Att: 18,718   Dacourt, Materazzi
3rd Round
Oct 28 vs Middlesbrough (a) 3-2 (aet.)
Att: 20,748   Ferguson, Bakayoko, Hutchison

4th Round
Nov 11 vs Sunderland (h) 1-1 (aet.)
*Att: 28,132   Collins
Sunderland won 5-4 on penalties*

EUROPEAN CUP
1970/71 SEASON
1st Round (1st leg)
Sep 16 vs Keflavik (h) 6-2
Att: 28,444   Ball 3, Royle 2, Kendall
1st Round (2nd leg)
Sep 30 vs Keflavik (a) 3-0 (aggregate 9-2)
Att: 9,500   Royle 2, Whittle
2nd Round (1st leg)
Oct 21 vs Bor. Moenchengladbach (a) 1-1
Att: 32,000   Kendall
2nd Round (2nd leg)
Nov 4 vs Bor. M'gladbach (h) 1-1 (aet.)
*Att: 42,744   Morrissey
Everton won 4-3 on penalties*
Quarter-Final (1st leg)
Mar 9 vs Panathinaikos (h) 1-1
Att: 46,047   Johnson
Quarter-Final (2nd leg)
Mar 24 vs Panathinaikos (a) 0-0 (agg. 1-1)
*Att: 25,000
Panathinaikos won on Away Goals*

EUROPEAN CUP-WINNERS-CUP
1984/85 SEASON
1st Round (1st leg)
Sep 19 vs University College Dublin (a) 0-0
Att: 9,750
1st Round (2nd leg)
Oct 2 vs Univ. College Dublin (h) 1-0
Att: 16,277   Sharp
2nd Round (1st leg)
Oct 24 vs Inter Bratislava (a) 1-0
Att: 15,000   Bracewell
2nd Round (2nd leg)
Nov 7 vs Inter Bratislava (h) 3-0 (agg. 4-0)
Att: 25,007   Heath, Sharp, Sheedy
Quarter-Final (1st leg)
Mar 6 vs Fortuna Sittard (h) 3-0
Att: 25,782   Gray 3
Quarter-Final (2nd leg)
Mar 20 vs Fortuna Sittard (a) 2-0 (agg. 5-0)
Att: 20,000   Reid, Sharp
Semi-Final (1st leg)
Apr 10 vs Bayern Munich (a) 0-0
Att: 67,000
Semi-Final (2nd leg)
Apr 24 vs Bayern Munich (h) 3-1 (agg. 3-1)
Att: 49,476   Sharp, Gray, Steven
FINAL (at Rotterdam)
May 15 vs Rapid Vienna 3-1
Att: 38,500   Gray, Steven, Sheedy

UEFA CUP
1975/76 SEASON
1st Round (1st leg)
Sep 17 vs AC Milan (h) 0-0
Att: 31,917
1st Round (2nd leg)
Oct 1 vs AC Milan (a) 0-1 (aggregate 0-1)
Att: 60,000

1978/79 SEASON
1st Round (1st leg)
Sep 12 vs Finn Harps (a) 5-0
*Att: 5,000   Thomas, King 2, Latchford,
Walsh*

1st Round (2nd leg)
Sep 26 vs Finn Harps (h) 5-0 (agg. 10-0)
*Att: 21,611   King, Latchford, Walsh, Ross,
Dobson*
2nd Round (1st leg)
Oct 18 vs Dukla Prague (h) 2-1
Att: 32,857   Latchford, King
2nd Round (2nd leg)
Nov 1 vs Dukla Prague (a) 0-1 (agg. 2-2)
*Att: 35,000
Dukla Prague won on Away Goals*

1979/80 SEASON
1st Round (1st leg)
Sep 19 vs Feyenoord (a) 0-1
Att: 40,000
1st Round (2nd leg)
Oct 3 vs Feyenoord (h) 0-1 (aggregate 0-2)
Att: 28,203

1974-75 SEASON

FIRST DIVISION

Derby County	42	21	11	10	67	49	53
Liverpool	42	20	11	11	60	39	51
Ipswich Town	42	23	5	14	66	44	51
Everton	**42**	**16**	**18**	**8**	**56**	**42**	**50**
Stoke City	42	17	15	10	64	48	49
Sheffield United	42	18	13	11	58	51	49
Middlesbrough	42	18	12	12	54	40	48
Manchester City	42	18	10	14	54	54	46
Leeds United	42	16	13	13	57	49	45
Burnley	42	17	11	14	68	67	45
Q.P.R.	42	16	10	16	54	54	42
Wolves	42	14	11	17	57	54	39
West Ham United	42	13	13	16	58	59	39
Coventry City	42	12	15	15	51	62	39
Newcastle United	42	15	9	18	59	72	39
Arsenal	42	13	11	18	47	49	37
Birmingham City	42	14	9	19	53	61	37
Leicester City	42	12	12	18	46	60	36
Tottenham Hotspur	42	13	8	21	52	63	34
Luton Town	42	11	11	20	47	65	33
Chelsea	42	9	15	18	42	72	33
Carlisle United	42	12	5	25	43	59	29

1975-76 SEASON

FIRST DIVISION

Liverpool	42	23	14	5	66	31	60
Q.P.R.	42	24	11	7	67	33	59
Manchester United	42	23	10	10	68	42	56
Derby County	42	21	11	10	75	58	53
Leeds United	42	21	9	12	65	46	51
Ipswich Town	42	16	14	12	54	48	46
Leicester City	42	13	19	10	48	51	45
Manchester City	42	16	12	15	64	46	43
Tottenham Hotspur	42	14	15	13	63	63	43
Norwich City	42	16	10	16	58	58	42
Everton	**42**	**15**	**12**	**15**	**60**	**66**	**42**
Stoke City	42	15	11	16	48	50	41
Middlesbrough	42	15	10	17	46	45	40
Coventry City	42	13	14	15	47	57	40
Newcastle United	42	15	9	18	71	62	39
Aston Villa	42	11	17	14	51	59	39
Arsenal	42	13	10	19	47	53	36
West Ham United	42	13	10	19	48	71	36
Birmingham City	42	13	7	22	57	75	33
Wolves	42	10	10	22	51	68	30
Burnley	42	9	10	23	43	66	28
Sheffield United	42	6	10	26	33	82	22

1976-77 SEASON

FIRST DIVISION

Liverpool	42	23	11	8	62	33	57
Manchester City	42	21	14	7	60	34	56
Ipswich Town	42	22	8	12	66	39	52
Aston Villa	42	22	7	13	76	50	51
Newcastle United	42	18	13	11	64	49	49
Manchester United	42	18	11	13	71	62	47
West Brom. Albion	42	16	13	13	62	56	45
Arsenal	42	16	11	15	64	59	43
Everton	**42**	**14**	**14**	**14**	**62**	**64**	**42**
Leeds United	42	15	12	15	48	51	42
Leicester City	42	12	18	12	47	60	42
Middlesbrough	42	14	13	15	40	45	41
Birmingham City	42	13	12	17	63	61	38
Q.P.R.	42	13	12	17	47	52	38
Derby County	42	9	19	14	50	55	37
Norwich City	42	14	9	19	47	64	37
West Ham United	42	11	14	17	46	65	36
Bristol City	42	11	13	18	38	48	35
Coventry City	42	10	15	17	48	59	35
Sunderland	42	11	12	19	46	54	34
Stoke City	42	10	14	18	28	51	34
Tottenham Hotspur	42	12	9	21	48	72	33

1977-78 SEASON

FIRST DIVISION

Nottingham Forest	42	25	14	3	69	24	64
Liverpool	42	24	9	9	65	34	57
Everton	**42**	**22**	**11**	**9**	**76**	**45**	**55**
Manchester City	42	20	12	10	74	51	52
Arsenal	42	21	10	11	60	37	52
West Brom. Albion	42	18	14	10	62	53	50
Coventry City	42	18	12	12	75	62	48
Aston Villa	42	18	10	14	57	42	46
Leeds United	42	18	10	14	63	53	46
Manchester United	42	16	10	16	67	63	42
Birmingham City	42	16	9	17	55	60	41
Derby County	42	14	13	15	54	59	41
Norwich City	42	11	18	13	52	66	40
Middlesbrough	42	12	15	15	42	54	39
Wolves	42	12	12	18	51	64	36
Chelsea	42	11	14	17	46	69	36
Bristol City	42	11	13	18	49	53	35
Ipswich Town	42	11	13	18	47	61	35
Q.P.R.	42	9	15	18	47	64	33
West Ham United	42	12	8	22	52	69	32
Newcastle United	42	6	10	26	42	78	22
Leicester City	42	5	12	25	26	70	22

1978-79 SEASON

FIRST DIVISION

Liverpool	42	30	8	4	85	16	68
Nottingham Forest	42	21	18	3	61	26	60
West Brom. Albion	42	24	11	7	72	35	59
Everton	**42**	**17**	**17**	**8**	**52**	**40**	**51**
Leeds United	42	18	14	10	70	52	50
Ipswich Town	42	20	9	13	63	49	49
Arsenal	42	17	14	11	61	48	48
Aston Villa	42	15	16	11	59	49	46
Manchester United	42	15	15	12	60	63	45
Coventry City	42	14	16	12	58	68	44
Tottenham Hotspur	42	13	15	14	48	61	41
Middlesbrough	42	15	10	17	57	50	40
Bristol City	42	15	10	17	47	51	40
Southampton	42	12	16	14	47	53	40
Manchester City	42	13	13	16	58	56	39
Norwich City	42	7	23	12	51	57	37
Bolton Wanderers	42	12	11	19	54	75	35
Wolves	42	13	8	21	44	68	34
Derby County	42	10	11	21	44	71	31
Q.P.R.	42	6	13	23	45	73	25
Birmingham City	42	6	10	26	37	64	22
Chelsea	42	5	10	27	44	92	20

1979-80 SEASON

FIRST DIVISION

Liverpool	42	25	10	7	81	30	60
Manchester United	42	24	10	8	65	35	58
Ipswich Town	42	22	9	11	68	39	53
Arsenal	42	18	16	8	52	36	52
Nottingham Forest	42	20	8	14	63	43	48
Wolves	42	19	9	14	58	47	47
Aston Villa	42	16	14	12	51	50	46
Southampton	42	18	9	15	65	53	45
Middlesbrough	42	16	12	14	50	44	44
West Brom. Albion	42	11	19	12	54	50	41
Leeds United	42	13	14	15	46	50	40
Norwich City	42	13	14	15	58	66	40
Crystal Palace	42	12	16	14	41	50	40
Tottenham Hotspur	42	15	10	17	52	62	40
Coventry City	42	16	7	19	56	66	39
Brighton & Hove Alb.	42	11	15	16	47	57	37
Manchester City	42	12	13	17	43	66	37
Stoke City	42	13	10	19	44	58	36
Everton	**42**	**9**	**17**	**16**	**43**	**51**	**35**
Bristol City	42	9	13	20	37	66	31
Derby County	42	11	8	23	47	67	30
Bolton Wanderers	42	5	15	22	38	73	25

1980-81 SEASON

FIRST DIVISION

Aston Villa	42	26	8	8	72	40	60
Ipswich Town	42	23	10	9	77	43	56
Arsenal	42	19	15	8	61	45	53
West Brom. Albion	42	20	12	10	60	42	52
Liverpool	42	17	17	8	62	46	51
Southampton	42	20	10	12	76	56	50
Nottingham Forest	42	19	12	11	62	45	50
Manchester United	42	15	18	9	51	36	48
Leeds United	42	17	10	15	39	47	44
Tottenham Hotspur	42	14	15	13	70	68	43
Stoke City	42	12	18	12	51	60	42
Manchester City	42	14	11	17	56	59	39
Birmingham City	42	13	12	17	50	61	38
Middlesbrough	42	16	5	21	53	51	37
Everton	**42**	**13**	**10**	**19**	**55**	**58**	**36**
Coventry City	42	13	10	19	48	68	36
Sunderland	42	14	7	21	58	53	35
Wolves	42	13	9	20	47	55	35
Brighton & Hove Alb.	42	14	7	21	54	67	35
Norwich City	42	13	7	22	49	73	33
Leicester City	42	13	6	23	40	67	32
Crystal Palace	42	6	7	29	47	83	19

1981-82 SEASON

FIRST DIVISION

Liverpool	42	26	9	7	80	32	87
Ipswich Town	42	26	5	11	75	53	83
Manchester United	42	22	12	8	59	29	78
Tottenham Hotspur	42	20	11	11	67	48	71
Arsenal	42	20	11	11	48	37	71
Swansea City	42	21	6	15	58	51	69
Southampton	42	19	9	14	72	67	66
Everton	**42**	**17**	**13**	**12**	**56**	**50**	**64**
West Ham United	42	14	16	12	66	57	58
Manchester City	42	15	13	14	49	50	58
Aston Villa	42	15	12	15	55	53	57
Nottingham Forest	42	15	12	15	42	48	57
Brighton & Hove Alb.	42	13	13	16	43	52	52
Coventry City	42	13	11	18	56	62	50
Notts County	42	13	8	21	45	69	47
Birmingham City	42	10	14	18	53	61	44
West Brom. Albion	42	11	11	20	46	57	44
Stoke City	42	12	8	22	44	63	44
Sunderland	42	11	11	20	38	58	44
Leeds United	42	10	12	20	39	61	42
Wolves	42	10	10	22	32	63	40
Middlesbrough	42	8	15	19	34	52	39

1982-83 SEASON

FIRST DIVISION

Liverpool	42	24	10	8	87	37	82
Watford	42	22	5	15	74	57	71
Manchester United	42	19	13	8	56	38	70
Tottenham Hotspur	42	20	9	13	65	50	69
Nottingham Forest	42	20	9	13	62	50	69
Aston Villa	42	21	5	16	62	50	68
Everton	**42**	**18**	**10**	**14**	**66**	**48**	**64**
West Ham United	42	20	4	18	68	62	64
Ipswich Town	42	15	13	14	64	50	58
Arsenal	42	16	10	16	58	56	58
West Brom. Albion	42	15	12	15	51	49	57
Southampton	42	15	12	15	54	58	57
Stoke City	42	16	9	17	53	64	57
Norwich City	42	14	12	16	52	58	54
Notts County	42	15	7	21	55	71	52
Sunderland	42	12	14	16	48	61	50
Birmingham City	42	12	15	16	40	55	50
Luton Town	42	12	13	17	65	84	49
Coventry City	42	13	9	20	48	59	48
Manchester City	42	13	8	21	47	70	47
Swansea City	42	10	11	21	51	69	41
Brighton & Hove Alb.	42	9	13	20	38	67	40

1983-84 SEASON

FIRST DIVISION

Liverpool	42	22	14	6	73	32	80
Southampton	42	22	11	9	66	38	77
Nottingham Forest	42	22	8	12	76	45	74
Manchester United	42	20	14	8	71	41	74
Q.P.R.	42	22	7	13	67	37	73
Arsenal	42	19	9	15	74	60	63
Everton	**42**	**16**	**14**	**12**	**44**	**42**	**62**
Tottenham Hotspur	42	17	10	15	64	65	61
West Ham United	42	17	9	16	60	55	60
Aston Villa	42	17	9	16	59	61	60
Watford	42	16	9	17	68	77	57
Ipswich Town	42	15	8	19	55	57	53
Sunderland	42	13	13	16	42	53	52
Norwich City	42	12	15	15	48	49	51
Leicester City	42	13	12	17	65	68	51
Luton Town	42	14	9	19	53	66	51
West Brom. Albion	42	14	9	19	48	62	51
Stoke City	42	13	11	18	44	63	50
Coventry City	42	13	11	18	57	77	50
Birmingham City	42	12	12	18	39	50	48
Notts County	42	10	11	21	50	72	41
Wolves	42	6	11	25	27	80	29

1984-85 SEASON

FIRST DIVISION

Everton	**42**	**28**	**6**	**8**	**88**	**43**	**90**
Liverpool	42	22	11	9	78	35	77
Tottenham Hotspur	42	23	8	11	78	51	77
Manchester United	42	22	10	10	77	47	76
Southampton	42	19	11	12	56	47	68
Chelsea	42	18	12	12	63	48	66
Arsenal	42	19	9	14	61	49	66
Sheffield Wednesday	42	17	14	11	58	45	65
Nottingham Forest	42	19	7	16	56	48	64
Aston Villa	42	15	11	16	60	60	56
Watford	42	14	13	15	81	71	55
West Brom	42	16	7	19	58	62	55
Luton Town	42	15	9	18	57	61	54
Newcastle United	42	13	13	16	55	70	52
Leicester City	42	15	6	21	65	73	51
West Ham United	42	13	12	17	51	68	51
Ipswich Town	42	13	11	18	46	57	50
Coventry City	42	15	5	22	47	64	50
Q.P.R.	42	13	11	18	53	72	50
Norwich City	42	13	10	19	46	64	49
Sunderland	42	10	10	22	40	62	40
Stoke City	42	3	8	31	24	91	17

1985-86 SEASON

FIRST DIVISION

Liverpool	42	26	10	6	89	37	88
Everton	**42**	**26**	**8**	**8**	**87**	**41**	**86**
West Ham United	42	26	6	10	74	40	84
Manchester United	42	22	10	10	70	36	76
Sheffield Wednesday	42	21	10	11	63	54	73
Chelsea	42	20	11	11	57	56	71
Arsenal	42	20	9	13	49	47	69
Nottingham Forest	42	19	11	12	69	53	68
Luton Town	42	18	12	12	61	44	66
Tottenham Hotspur	42	19	8	15	74	52	65
Newcastle United	42	17	12	13	67	72	63
Watford	42	16	11	15	69	62	59
Q.P.R.	42	15	7	20	53	64	52
Southampton	42	12	10	20	51	62	46
Manchester City	42	11	12	19	43	57	45
Aston Villa	42	10	14	18	51	67	44
Coventry City	42	11	10	21	48	71	43
Oxford United	42	10	12	20	62	80	42
Leicester City	42	10	12	20	54	76	42
Ipswich Town	42	11	8	23	32	55	41
Birmingham City	42	8	5	29	30	73	29
West Brom	42	4	12	26	35	89	24

1986-87 SEASON

FIRST DIVISION

Everton	**42**	**26**	**8**	**8**	**76**	**31**	**86**
Liverpool	42	23	8	11	72	42	77
Tottenham Hotspur	42	21	8	13	68	43	71
Arsenal	42	20	10	12	58	35	70
Norwich City	42	17	17	8	53	51	68
Wimbledon	42	19	9	14	57	50	66
Luton Town	42	18	12	12	47	45	66
Nottingham Forest	42	18	11	13	64	51	65
Watford	42	18	9	15	67	54	63
Coventry City	42	17	12	13	50	45	63
Manchester United	42	14	14	14	52	45	56
Southampton	42	14	10	18	69	68	52
Sheffield Wednesday	42	13	13	16	58	59	52
Chelsea	42	13	13	16	53	64	52
West Ham United	42	14	10	18	52	67	52
Q.P.R.	42	13	11	18	48	64	50
Newcastle United	42	12	11	19	47	65	47
Oxford United	42	11	13	18	44	69	46
Charlton Athletic	42	11	11	20	45	55	44
Leicester City	42	11	9	22	54	76	42
Manchester City	42	8	15	19	36	57	39
Aston Villa	42	8	12	22	45	79	36

1987-88 SEASON

FIRST DIVISION

Liverpool	40	26	12	2	87	24	90
Manchester United	40	23	12	5	71	38	81
Nottingham Forest	40	20	13	7	67	39	73
Everton	**40**	**19**	**13**	**8**	**53**	**27**	**70**
Q.P.R.	40	19	10	11	48	38	67
Arsenal	40	18	12	10	58	39	66
Wimbledon	40	14	15	11	58	47	57
Newcastle United	40	14	14	12	55	53	56
Luton Town	40	14	11	15	57	58	53
Coventry City	40	13	14	13	46	53	53
Sheffield Wednesday	40	15	8	17	52	66	53
Southampton	40	12	14	14	49	53	50
Tottenham Hotspur	40	12	11	17	38	48	47
Norwich City	40	12	9	19	40	52	45
Derby County	40	10	13	17	35	45	43
West Ham United	40	9	15	16	40	52	42
Charlton Athletic	40	9	15	16	38	52	42
Chelsea	40	9	15	16	50	68	42
Portsmouth	40	7	14	19	36	66	35
Watford	40	7	11	22	27	51	32
Oxford United	40	6	13	21	44	80	31

1988-89 SEASON

FIRST DIVISION

Arsenal	38	22	10	6	73	36	76
Liverpool	38	22	10	6	65	28	76
Nottingham Forest	38	17	13	8	64	43	64
Norwich City	38	17	11	10	48	45	62
Derby County	38	17	7	14	40	38	58
Tottenham Hotspur	38	15	12	11	60	46	57
Coventry City	38	14	13	11	47	42	55
Everton	**38**	**14**	**12**	**12**	**50**	**45**	**54**
Q.P.R.	38	14	11	13	43	37	53
Millwall	38	14	11	13	47	52	53
Manchester United	38	13	12	13	45	35	51
Wimbledon	38	14	9	15	50	46	51
Southampton	38	10	15	13	52	66	45
Charlton Athletic	38	10	12	16	44	58	42
Sheffield Wednesday	38	10	12	16	34	51	42
Luton Town	38	10	11	17	42	52	41
Aston Villa	38	9	13	16	45	56	40
Middlesbrough	38	9	12	17	44	61	39
West Ham United	38	10	8	20	37	62	38
Newcastle United	38	7	10	21	32	63	31

1989-90 SEASON

FIRST DIVISION

Liverpool	38	23	10	5	78	37	79
Aston Villa	38	21	7	10	57	38	70
Tottenham Hotspur	38	19	6	13	59	47	63
Arsenal	38	18	8	12	54	38	62
Chelsea	38	16	12	10	58	50	60
Everton	**38**	**17**	**8**	**13**	**51**	**33**	**59**
Southampton	38	15	10	13	71	63	55
Wimbledon	38	13	16	9	47	40	55
Nottingham Forest	38	15	9	14	55	47	54
Norwich City	38	13	14	11	44	42	53
Q.P.R.	38	13	11	14	45	44	50
Coventry City	38	14	7	17	39	59	49
Manchester United	38	13	9	16	46	47	48
Manchester City	38	12	12	14	43	52	48
Crystal Palace	38	13	9	16	42	66	48
Derby County	38	13	7	18	43	40	46
Luton Town	38	10	13	15	43	57	43
Sheffield Wednesday	38	11	10	17	35	51	43
Charlton Athletic	38	7	9	22	31	57	30
Millwall	38	5	11	22	39	65	26

1990-91 SEASON

FIRST DIVISION

Arsenal	38	24	13	1	74	18	83
Liverpool	38	23	7	8	77	40	76
Crystal Palace	38	20	9	9	50	41	69
Leeds United	38	19	7	12	65	47	64
Manchester City	38	17	11	10	64	53	62
Manchester United	38	16	12	10	58	45	59
Wimbledon	38	14	14	10	53	46	56
Nottingham Forest	38	14	12	12	65	50	54
Everton	**38**	**13**	**12**	**13**	**50**	**46**	**51**
Tottenham	38	11	16	11	51	50	49
Chelsea	38	13	10	15	58	69	49
Q.P.R.	38	12	10	16	44	53	46
Sheffield United	38	13	7	18	36	55	46
Southampton	38	12	9	17	58	69	45
Norwich City	38	13	6	19	41	64	45
Coventry City	38	11	11	16	42	49	44
Aston Villa	38	9	14	15	46	58	41
Luton Town	38	10	7	21	42	61	37
Sunderland	38	8	10	20	38	60	34
Derby County	38	5	9	24	37	75	24

Arsenal 2 points deducted
Manchester United 1 point deducted

1991-92 SEASON

FIRST DIVISION

Leeds United	42	22	16	4	74	37	82
Manchester United	42	21	15	6	63	33	78
Sheffield Wednesday	42	21	12	9	62	49	75
Arsenal	42	19	15	8	81	46	72
Manchester City	42	20	10	12	61	48	70
Liverpool	42	16	16	10	47	40	64
Aston Villa	42	17	9	16	48	44	60
Nottingham Forest	42	16	11	15	60	58	59
Sheffield United	42	16	9	17	65	63	57
Crystal Palace	42	14	15	13	53	61	57
Q.P.R.	42	12	18	12	48	47	54
Everton	**42**	**13**	**14**	**15**	**52**	**51**	**53**
Wimbledon	42	13	14	15	53	53	53
Chelsea	42	13	14	15	50	60	53
Tottenham	42	15	7	20	58	63	52
Southampton	42	14	10	18	39	55	52
Oldham Athletic	42	14	9	19	63	67	51
Norwich City	42	11	12	19	47	63	45
Coventry City	42	11	11	20	35	44	44
Luton Town	42	10	12	20	38	71	42
Notts County	42	10	10	22	40	62	40
West Ham United	42	9	11	22	37	59	38

1992-93 SEASON

PREMIER DIVISION

Manchester United	42	24	12	6	67	31	84
Aston Villa	42	21	11	10	57	40	74
Norwich City	42	21	9	12	61	65	72
Blackburn Rovers	42	20	11	11	68	46	71
Q.P.R.	42	17	12	13	63	55	63
Liverpool	42	16	11	15	62	55	59
Sheffield Wednesday	42	15	14	13	55	51	59
Tottenham	42	16	11	15	60	66	59
Manchester City	42	15	12	15	56	51	57
Arsenal	42	15	11	16	40	38	56
Chelsea	42	14	14	14	51	54	56
Wimbledon	42	14	12	16	56	55	54
Everton	**42**	**15**	**8**	**19**	**53**	**55**	**53**
Sheffield United	42	14	10	18	54	53	52
Coventry City	42	13	13	16	52	57	52
Ipswich Town	42	12	16	14	50	55	52
Leeds United	42	12	15	15	57	62	51
Southampton	42	13	11	18	54	61	50
Oldham Athletic	42	13	10	19	63	74	49
Crystal Palace	42	11	16	15	48	61	49
Middlesbrough	42	11	11	20	54	75	44
Nottingham Forest	42	10	10	22	41	62	40

1993-94 SEASON

F.A. PREMIERSHIP

Manchester United	42	27	11	4	80	38	92
Blackburn Rovers	42	25	9	8	63	36	84
Newcastle United	42	23	8	11	82	41	77
Arsenal	42	18	17	7	53	28	71
Leeds United	42	18	16	8	65	39	70
Wimbledon	42	18	11	13	56	53	65
Sheffield Wednesday	42	16	16	10	76	54	64
Liverpool	42	17	9	16	59	55	60
Q.P.R.	42	16	12	14	62	64	60
Aston Villa	42	15	12	15	46	50	57
Coventry City	42	14	14	14	43	45	56
Norwich City	42	12	17	13	65	61	53
West Ham United	42	13	13	16	47	58	52
Chelsea	42	13	12	17	49	53	51
Tottenham Hotspur	42	11	12	19	54	59	45
Manchester City	42	9	18	15	38	49	45
Everton	**42**	**12**	**8**	**22**	**42**	**63**	**44**
Southampton	42	12	7	23	49	66	43
Ipswich Town	42	9	16	17	35	58	43
Sheffield United	42	8	18	16	42	60	42
Oldham Athletic	42	9	13	20	42	68	40
Swindon Town	42	5	15	22	47	100	30

1994-95 SEASON

F.A. PREMIERSHIP

Blackburn Rovers	42	27	8	7	80	39	89
Manchester United	42	26	10	6	77	28	88
Nottingham Forest	42	22	11	9	72	43	77
Liverpool	42	21	11	10	65	37	74
Leeds United	42	20	13	9	59	38	63
Newcastle United	42	20	12	10	67	47	72
Tottenham Hotspur	42	16	14	12	66	58	62
Q.P.R.	42	17	9	16	61	59	60
Wimbledon	42	15	11	16	48	65	56
Southampton	42	12	18	12	61	63	54
Chelsea	42	13	15	14	50	55	54
Arsenal	42	13	12	17	52	49	51
Sheffield Wednesday	42	13	12	17	49	57	51
West Ham United	42	13	11	18	44	48	50
Everton	**42**	**11**	**17**	**14**	**44**	**51**	**50**
Coventry City	42	12	14	16	44	62	50
Manchester City	42	12	13	17	53	64	49
Aston Villa	42	11	15	16	51	56	48
Crystal Palace	42	11	12	19	34	49	45
Norwich City	42	10	13	19	37	54	43
Leicester City	42	6	11	25	45	80	29
Ipswich Town	42	7	6	29	36	93	27

1995-96 SEASON

F.A. PREMIERSHIP

Manchester United	38	25	7	6	73	35	82
Newcastle United	38	24	6	8	66	37	78
Liverpool	38	20	11	7	70	34	71
Aston Villa	38	18	9	11	52	35	63
Arsenal	38	17	12	9	49	32	63
Everton	**38**	**17**	**10**	**11**	**64**	**44**	**61**
Blackburn Rovers	38	18	7	13	61	47	61
Tottenham Hotspur	38	16	13	9	50	38	61
Nottingham Forest	38	15	13	10	50	54	58
West Ham United	38	14	9	15	43	52	51
Chelsea	38	12	14	12	46	44	50
Middlesbrough	38	11	10	17	35	50	43
Leeds United	38	12	7	19	40	57	43
Wimbledon	38	10	11	17	55	70	41
Sheffield Wednesday	38	10	10	18	48	61	40
Coventry City	38	8	14	16	42	60	38
Southampton	38	9	11	18	34	52	38
Manchester City	38	9	11	18	33	58	38
Q.P.R.	38	9	6	23	38	57	33
Bolton Wanderers	38	8	5	25	39	71	29

1996-97 SEASON

F.A PREMIERSHIP

Manchester United	38	21	12	5	76	44	75
Newcastle United	38	19	11	8	73	40	68
Arsenal	38	19	11	8	62	32	68
Liverpool	38	19	11	8	62	37	68
Aston Villa	38	17	10	11	47	34	61
Chelsea	38	16	11	11	58	55	59
Sheffield Wednesday	38	14	15	9	50	51	57
Wimbledon	38	15	11	12	49	46	56
Leicester City	38	12	11	15	46	54	47
Tottenham Hotspur	38	13	7	18	44	51	46
Leeds United	38	11	13	14	28	38	46
Derby County	38	11	13	14	45	58	46
Blackburn Rovers	38	9	15	14	42	43	42
West Ham United	38	10	12	16	39	48	42
Everton	**38**	**10**	**12**	**16**	**44**	**57**	**42**
Southampton	38	10	11	17	50	56	41
Coventry City	38	9	14	15	38	54	41
Sunderland	38	10	10	18	35	53	40
Middlesbrough	38	10	12	16	51	60	39
Nottingham Forest	38	6	16	16	31	59	34

1997-98 SEASON

F.A. PREMIERSHIP

Arsenal	38	23	9	6	68	33	78
Manchester United	38	23	8	7	73	26	77
Liverpool	38	18	11	9	68	42	65
Chelsea	38	20	3	15	71	43	63
Leeds United	38	17	8	13	57	46	59
Blackburn Rovers	38	16	10	12	57	52	58
Aston Villa	38	17	6	15	49	48	57
West Ham United	38	16	8	14	56	57	56
Derby County	38	16	7	15	52	49	55
Leicester City	38	13	14	11	51	41	53
Coventry City	38	12	16	10	46	44	52
Southampton	38	14	6	18	50	55	48
Newcastle United	38	11	11	16	35	44	44
Tottenham Hotspur	38	11	11	16	44	56	44
Wimbledon	38	10	14	14	34	46	44
Sheffield Wednesday	38	12	8	18	52	67	44
Everton	**38**	**9**	**13**	**16**	**41**	**56**	**40**
Bolton Wanderers	38	9	13	16	41	61	40
Barnsley	38	10	5	23	37	82	35
Crystal Palace	38	8	9	21	37	71	33

1998-99 SEASON

F.A. PREMIERSHIP

Manchester United	38	22	13	3	80	37	79
Arsenal	38	22	12	4	59	17	78
Chelsea	38	20	15	3	57	30	75
Leeds United	38	18	13	7	62	34	67
West Ham United	38	16	9	13	46	53	57
Aston Villa	38	15	10	13	51	46	55
Liverpool	38	15	9	14	68	49	54
Derby County	38	13	13	12	40	45	52
Middlesbrough	38	12	15	11	48	54	51
Leicester City	38	12	13	13	40	46	49
Tottenham Hotspur	38	11	14	13	47	50	47
Sheffield Wednesday	38	13	7	18	41	42	46
Newcastle United	38	11	13	14	48	54	46
Everton	**38**	**11**	**10**	**17**	**42**	**47**	**43**
Coventry City	38	11	9	18	39	51	42
Wimbledon	38	10	12	16	40	63	42
Southampton	38	11	8	19	37	64	41
Charlton Athletic	38	8	12	18	41	56	36
Blackburn Rovers	38	7	14	17	38	52	35
Nottingham Forest	38	7	9	22	35	69	30